USELESS KNOWLEDGE

GENERAL

WHO WHAT WHERE WHEN

150 Answers to Questions You Never Thought to Ask

PIL

Publications International, Ltd.

Cover Images: Artbeats, Shutterstock.com

Interior Images: Art Explosion: 21, 28, 97, 122, 132, 145, 213, 217, 234, 254, 264; Clipart.com: 66, 86; Shutterstock.com: 7, 17, 50

Contributing writers: Angelique Anacleto, Brett Ballantini, Diane Lanzillotta Bobis, Joshua D. Boeringa, Shelley Bueché, Michelle Burton, Steve Cameron, Matt Clark, Anthony G. Craine, Dan Dalton, Paul Forrester, Shanna Freeman, Chuck Giamatta, Ed Grabianowski, Jack Greer, Tom Harris, Vickey Kalambakal, Brett Kyle, Noah Liberman, Letty Livingston, Alex Nechas, Jessica Royer Ocken, Thad Plumley, ArLynn Leiber Presser, Pat Sherman, William Wagner, Carrie Williford

ISBN: 978-1-4508-9334-3

Manufactured in U.S.A.

8 7 6 5 4 3 2 1

CONTENTS

Chapter 1
BATTLE OF THE SEXES

Q Why are women called the fairer sex?

A "The female body is a work of art," Elaine says in an episode of *Seinfeld*. "The male body is utilitarian; it's for gettin' around, like a jeep." When Jerry asks her if she finds the male body unattractive, Elaine admits, "It's hideous. The hair, the lumpiness—it's simian." There's no getting around it: If art museums and beer commercials—and sitcoms, of course—are any indication, the female form is the one we think is fairer.

Nobody knows the origin of the phrase "the fairer sex," but recent scientific research indicates that whoever coined it was right on the money. Even when we consider meanings of "fair" beyond "pretty" or "attractive," it seems that women have cornered the market.

Think about your typical Hollywood love story. When the hunky male lead finally sweeps the swooning ingénue off her feet and gives her that first long romantic kiss, note the difference in the skin tones of their faces: The man is invariably darker than the woman. Filmmakers have always known what science is now confirming: From adolescence on, a woman's complexion is lighter than a man's. It's true in many different populations around the world, and it can be explained by the fact that women have more subcutaneous fat (that is, fat directly beneath the skin). This fat protects the skin from the sex hormones that increase pigmentation, keeping women's skin fairer than men's.

But let's take it one step further. Women may also be fairer in another sense. A policy research report prepared for the World Bank in 1999 suggests that the presence of women in governments may make those ruling bodies more equitable. In "Are Women Really the 'Fairer' Sex? Corruption and Women in Government," economists David Dollar (a guy born to work for the World Bank), Raymond Fisman, and Roberta Gatti point to a growing body of research demonstrating that women are less selfish and more ethical than men.

Armed with this data, they took standardized ratings of government corruption around the world and compared them to the numbers of women participating in those governments. They found that the more women were involved in a government, the better its score tended to be on the corruption scale.

We won't argue with science, but we have our own, simpler theory about why women are called the fairer sex: They're soft and they smell good.

Q Why do men leave the seat up?

A Ever since Eve bit the apple, human history has been a battle between the sexes. But it wasn't until the late eighteenth century that men and women were given the weapon they needed to turn the battle into a war: In 1775, Alexander Cummings invented the flush toilet. Since then, the toilet seat has done more damage to marriages than strip clubs, charge cards, and mothers-in-law combined. Men and women each make a convincing argument in the Great Toilet Seat Debate. Men ask: Why should we always be responsible for putting the seat up and down? Shouldn't women raise the toilet seat when they're finished?

Women counter: We already do enough work around the house, and the disgusting risk of sitting on a urine-damp rim (or worse, falling into the toilet) far outweighs the minor inconvenience of raising and lowering a toilet seat. Why can't men simply put the seat down?

At first blush, the answer seems obvious: Men are inherently lazy. But perhaps what women consider "lazy," men call "efficient."

Indeed, some biologists argue that a number of human attributes have developed from the evolutionary imperative to conserve energy. These include a little trait known as bipedalism. This "energy efficiency" paradigm argues that the conservation of energy is necessary and beneficial to the survival of mankind. So it's possible that men leave the toilet seat up because they are conserving energy for the next evolutionary step of humankind. We don't know what this next step will be exactly, but it will undoubtedly involve a couch and a flat-screen TV.

Well, great. This explanation, however, does nothing for the woman whose nighttime trip to the bathroom is fraught with peril. Fortunately, whenever such a dilemma is raised (or lowered), you can bet it's been the subject of an academic paper.

Sure enough, several academicians have addressed the issue. Richard Harter, a retired mathematician from South Dakota (the mathematics business apparently is slow in South Dakota), tackled the problem in a 1998 paper. After factoring such variables as the likelihood of the woman agreeing to raise the toilet seat when she's finished ("none"), Harter concluded the most efficient and fair solution is for the man to put the seat down exactly half the time. In 2007, economist Hammad Al-Sabah Siddiqi, from the Lahore University of Management Sciences in Pakistan, jumped into the fray. Siddiqi argued that because of wifely nagging, the social norm is to leave the toilet seat down, despite this being far less efficient than leaving it up.

There seems to be no end in sight to the battle of bathroom behavior. Too bad. If the sexes could forge a toilet-seat truce, they could focus on something important: bickering about the in-laws.

Q Why do men's and women's shirts have buttons on opposite sides?

A Despite the many strides the feminist movement has made over the past few decades, there is simply no denying that men and women are biologically different. Clothing has developed in ways to accommodate these differences. Some make sense (we'd wager that you've never seen women's underwear sporting that little flap/vent thing). But putting buttons on opposite sides of the shirt? Why?

Although it might seem ridiculous for men's and women's shirts to have buttons on opposite sides—most people are right-handed, and it is far easier to manipulate a button with your dominant hand—scholars point to fashion history to explain how this came to be.

Buttons have been around for thousands of years, but they served no purpose other than being decorative until about the thirteenth century. That's when the functional button (and just as importantly, the buttonhole) was invented, sending European nobility into a veritable button frenzy. Buttons became a symbol of both status and fashion, appearing everywhere and anywhere, often unnecessarily.

Perhaps the apex of button mania came in the sixteenth century with the button-loving king of France, Francis I. In 1520, Francis I planned a meeting with the English king, Henry VIII, in hopes of arranging a military alliance. Wanting desperately to impress Henry VIII, Francis I thought long and hard about how to strike the right chord.

It was the sort of situation that required the utmost tact and statesmanship; the sort of situation that needed the grace and intelligence befitting the ruler of one of the world's greatest powers; the sort of situation, Francis I tragically decided, that demanded he wear a velvet suit adorned with more than thirteen thousand gold buttons. There is no record of Henry VIII's reaction, though it goes without saying that no alliance was formed.

Francis I's ill-fated wardrobe decision also gives us insight into our original question. For a long time, buttons were too costly to appear on anything except the garments of the nobility. Because noble ladies were dressed by their servants, it was the obvious choice to put the buttons on the left side, making it easier for the right-handed servants to button their mistresses. Men dressed themselves, and so their buttons went on the right.

According to historians, there is no real reason for men's and women's buttons to persist in their opposition—it continues out of tradition. Thankfully, that's the only button tradition Francis I and his contemporaries bequeathed to us.

Q Why won't men ask for directions?

A The stereotype that men refuse to ask for directions has been fertile territory for amateur comedians over the years; at the same time, experience seems to suggest that there may be some truth to it. In fact, we suspect plenty of women—perhaps some who are reading this right now, as they are being driven farther and farther away from their destinations by men who insist they are not lost—are eagerly awaiting the answer to this question.

Though it might be small consolation, researchers have claimed to have evidence that suggests men's disinclination to ask for directions may be because they have a better chance of not getting lost in the first place. According to a 2000 study in *Nature Neuroscience,* men might have trouble asking for directions simply because they are naturally better than women at finding their way around. The study, which examined men's and women's brain responses to spatial puzzles, found that the left hippocampal region—the part of the brain involved in spatial problems—activated more frequently and intensely in men than in women. Accordingly, men were consistently better than women at solving spatial and directional puzzles. The study posits that men use more geometric or spatial cues to find their way, while women tend to use landmarks. (Which helps explain why women more frequently say, "Go left at the McDonald's," while men tend to say, "Head east on Main Street" when providing directions.)

How did this develop? For the answer, we look to socio-biologists, evolutionary experts who attempt to explain biological traits based on evolutionary theory; in particular, natural selection. According to socio-biologists, men developed better neural compasses because way back in their chest-beating, club-wielding caveman days, males foraged far and wide for food for their families, while females stayed in the caves, tending to the youngsters. Better foragers—with a better sense of direction—not only had increased chances of survival, but also proved more attractive as potential mates; thus, the genes for "direction" were passed on.

So, ladies, the next time your husband claims that he's not lost, give him a break. There's a chance he just can't help it. Now, if only those socio-biologists could figure out why men can't put the toilet seat down.

Q Why does the woman take the man's last name when they marry?

A It once was a given that a woman would take her husband's last name—patriarchal traditions in English-speaking countries gave her little choice.

A typical family unit placed the man as the head of the household, with both responsibility for and authority over his wife and children. When a girl was born, she became a member of her father's line and was given his last name. Upon marrying, her primary roles became those of wife and the mother of her husband's children. She also became her husband's responsibility and often was considered his property. It stood to reason, then, that she would assume his last name.

Most people in England didn't even have last names until the eleventh century; they typically were known by first names and by their professions or titles. Nobility and royalty began to adopt last names to determine property and title succession around the time of the Domesday Book, a survey of English citizens that was completed in 1086. The practice of passing last names through the father's family trickled down to the lower classes and became the standard in lands colonized and ruled by England.

As the roles of women evolved, so did the practice of automatically taking the man's last name upon marriage. In the 1850s, American suffragist Lucy Stone first raised the issue of married women retaining their last names, also known as maiden names. A few women followed her suggestion, but most hewed to tradition. As increasing numbers of women forged professional careers and identities away from the home in the twentieth century, more kept their maiden names after marriage. By the 1980s, about 20 percent of married women were retaining their unmarried last names.

But the trend is swinging back the other way. Today, about 10 percent of women keep their maiden names after marriage. Some women hyphenate it with their husband's last name; some couples choose a completely different last name; and in rare instances, a husband will take the last name of his wife. How's that for progress?

Q What did cowgirls do in the Old West?

A Here's one thing they didn't do: spend a lot of time chatting with biographers. Although it's generally acknowledged that there were plenty of women whose work was indispensable on the ranches of the American frontier—just like their more glorified male counterparts—their travails are not well documented. It wasn't until the late nineteenth century that cowgirls came into their own, and by then the Old West was fading into history.

The cowgirls who achieved their fame in the 1890s did just about everything that the cowboys of the day did: They competed and performed in public, demonstrating their riding, roping, and trick shooting skills. And that's it. Gone were the days of driving herds across the dusty plains; cowboys and cowgirls had become rough-and-tumble entertainers. True cow-folk were a thing of the past.

The genuine cowboy lifestyle flourished for only about twenty-five years, from the end of the Civil War in 1865 until around 1890. This is when cattle ranching on the Western frontier was extremely lucrative—it's when small groups of men rounded up herds, watched over them in the open country, and drove them hundreds of miles to railroads so that they could be shipped to cities for butchering. But it didn't last. Farms took over the range, barbed wire fences enclosed the herds, and ranches were built close to railroads. Consequently, long drives became unnecessary.

Even as the lifestyle was disappearing, the Old West was being romanticized and cowboys were becoming larger-than-life heroes. Their independence and freedom inspired a nation that felt more and more constrained by city life and industrial drudgery. Wild

West shows like Buffalo Bill Cody's began to appear—they were hugely popular events in which large casts of performers entertained crowds with trick riding, roping, and other cowboy feats that evoked the rugged freedom of the plains.

And this is where cowgirls first appeared. Although women had carried much of the burden of ranch work in the Old West, they weren't doing the glamorized jobs of the cowboys. But once cowboys became entertainers rather than laborers, talented women could join in the fun.

The most famous cowgirl of her day was Lucille Mulhall. Born in 1885, Mulhall honed her skills while growing up on her family's ranch in Oklahoma. On her way to becoming the women's world champion in roping and tying wild steers, she appeared frequently in her father's Wild West show and was, for a time, the featured performer from an all-star cast in the Miller Brothers' 101 Ranch Real Wild West Show. Will Rogers dubbed her the "world's first cowgirl," which probably came as news to women like Annie Oakley, who had been performing in Wild West shows for years.

Then there was Fannie Sperry Steele, who was born in 1887 in Montana. Steele was a world champion bronc rider and could also handle firearms with aplomb. After establishing herself as a rodeo star, she and her husband put together their own touring Wild West show. Steele remained active past age seventy, running a guest ranch in Montana.

Steele lived long enough to see herself become immortalized. In 1978, she was inducted into the National Cowgirl Museum and Hall of Fame in Fort Worth, Texas, where what little history there is of cowgirls is lovingly collected and preserved.

Chapter 2
GRAB BAG

Q Do farmers really need that extra hour of Daylight Savings Time?

A Sure, go and blame farmers because you lose a whole hour of sleep every spring. It's a common misconception that Daylight Saving Time (DST) was created to help farmers. The truth is, they're none too pleased about it either.

You see, cows and crops don't really care what the clock says. They're on "God's Time," otherwise known as Apparent Solar Time. When the sun's up, they're up. And when the clock is set an hour later, farmers lose a whole hour of morning productivity.

So if you can't point your tired little finger at the farmers, then who is responsible? Well, it was Benjamin Franklin who first proposed the idea of "saving daylight." While serving as the American delegate to France in 1784, he wrote an essay titled "An Economical Project for Diminishing the Cost of Light." In it, the thrifty Franklin discussed resetting clocks to make the most use of natural daylight hours.

This, he said, could save Parisian families "an immense sum" per year in the cost of tallow and wax for evening candles.

Though many were intrigued (and amused) by Franklin's essay, the concept of daylight saving didn't take hold until more than a century later, when Englishman William Willett presented it again in his pamphlet "The Waste of Daylight" (1907). When World War I began, the British Parliament enacted DST throughout England to reduce the need for artificial lighting and save fuel.

In 1918, the U.S. Congress followed suit, placing America on DST to conserve resources for the remainder of the war. Even back then, DST was widely unpopular. The law was repealed in 1919 and not observed again until WWII, when President Roosevelt instituted year-round DST, called "War Time," from 1942 to 1945.

From 1945 to 1966 there were no U.S. laws regarding DST. This meant that states and local towns were free to observe DST—or not. How did anyone know what time *Bonanza* was on? Suffice it to say, there was plenty of confusion.

Congress took action in 1966, enacting the Uniform Time Act to establish consistent timelines across the country. But any area that wanted to remain exempt from DST could do so by passing a local ordinance.

The Energy Policy Act of 2005 extended DST, beginning in 2007, to the time it is currently: It begins at 2:00 A.M. on the second Sunday in March and ends at 2:00 A.M. on the first Sunday in November. Proponents of DST say that it saves energy and prevents traffic accidents and crimes while providing extra daylight time for outdoor activities. Still, DST has its share of detractors.

The farming state of Indiana—one of the last states to adopt statewide DST, in April 2006—has fueled the DST debate. A 2007 study by Matthew Kotchen and Laura Grant of the University of Santa Barbara concluded that enacting DST in Indiana actually increased electricity consumption in the state, costing Indiana households an additional $8.6 million in 2007.

So, does DST conserve energy, as was originally intended? Well, it seems that DST has us turning off the evening lights but cranking up the AC. Inventive as he was, Benjamin Franklin never foresaw that.

Q Can a person really be intelligent but not smart?

A Very bright people are capable of doing some very dimwitted things. Take Eliot Spitzer. The former governor and attorney general of New York may have had an up-and-coming political career and a degree from Harvard, but that didn't stop him from getting caught in the middle of a high-priced prostitution ring.

And what about the heads of the "Big Three" North American automakers? In the midst of 2008's economic crisis, they traveled to Washington, D.C., to beg for twenty-five billion dollars of the taxpayers' money. The thing is, each of these guys flew to D.C. on his own private jet. Might have been a smart time to go coach.

Shouldn't these highly successful, highly intelligent people have known better? One would think so. But leading industrial psychologist Mortimer Feinberg says that the dark side of being bright is that one can actually be sabotaged by one's own intellect. In his book *Why Smart People Do Dumb Things: Lessons from the New Science of Behavioral Economics*, Feinberg explains: "Intelligent people run the risk of self-destruction caused by their own brilliance. That self-destruction is caused by a virus that flourishes within strong intellects. And there is no escape. If you possess above-average intelligence you already have the virus. It comes with the high IQ territory."

The virus is what Feinberg calls Self-Destructive Intelligence Syndrome. And people who have it often fall prey to one of what he calls the Four Pillars of Stupidity: There's hubris (pride to the point that one no longer fears public opinion); arrogance (feeling entitled to anything and everything one wants); narcissism (self-absorption to the point that one is blind to reality); and the unconscious need to fail (apparently, some highly intelligent people just can't handle the pressure of being so brainy).

Perhaps this helps to shed some light on what happened to Stephen Chao. In 1992, the Harvard MBA and media-biz whiz was climbing the ranks as the newly crowned president of Fox News. But that didn't prevent him from making a huge, lame-brained blunder. Invited to speak at a management conference for Fox executives, board members, and world dignitaries—including Fox owner Rupert Murdoch, U.S. defense secretary Dick Cheney, and National Endowment for the Humanities chairwoman Lynne Cheney—Chao decided that it would be a fabulous idea to hire a male stripper to perform in the middle of his talk. (The topic was censorship, after all.)

And so the stripper took off his clothes (right beside Lynne Cheney, as fate would have it), and Chao was immediately fired. Things went even further south for him from there—he ended up working at McDonald's for a while. But, hey, he was hardly the first person of high intelligence to crash and burn. Sometimes it takes real brains to be so brainless.

Q Has anyone jumped off the Golden Gate Bridge and lived to tell about it?

A Yes, more than two dozen people have survived the fall. That sounds like a lot—until you learn that more than 1,300 have taken the leap since the bridge opened in 1937.

With a success rate like that, the twenty-one-story drop is one of the more effective suicide methods. It's also one of the nastiest. After four seconds hurtling through the air (just enough time for a change of heart), the jumper hits the water at seventy-five miles per hour. In most cases, the force of the impact—fifteen thousand pounds per square inch—will break the jumper's ribs and vertebrae. The broken ribs usually pierce the lungs, spleen, and heart, and cause massive internal bleeding. If a jumper somehow survives, he or she likely will drown.

A handful of jumpers lived to tell the tale because they hit the water feet first. Kevin Hines jumped and survived in 2000, when he was 19 years old. Immediately after taking the leap, he changed his mind and prayed to survive. In the rapid fall, he managed to turn himself so that he hit feet first. Hitting vertically helped Hines's body penetrate the water, reducing the force of impact. The force was great enough to break his back and shatter his vertebrae, but none of his organs were punctured. In 1979, a man survived in good enough shape—his worst injury was several cracked vertebrae—to

swim ashore and drive to a hospital.

There is roughly one documented jump from the bridge every two weeks, making it the most popular suicide spot in the world. (There likely are other cases in which no one saw the jumper and the body washed out to sea.) The bridge is a jumping hotspot for two reasons: First, some people see it as romantic to leap from such a beautiful structure into the water; second, it's incredibly easy to do. The bridge has a pedestrian walkway, and all that stands between a suicidal person and the plunge is a four-foot railing. One possible explanation for this short railing is that the chief engineer of the bridge, Joseph Strauss, was only five feet tall and wanted to be able to enjoy the view.

Over the years, calls to add a barrier to the Golden Gate Bridge have been met with resistance in San Francisco. Opponents declare that the money would be better spent elsewhere; they object to compromising the beauty of the bridge to stop people from attempting suicide, since these people would likely just resort to a different method.

In October 2008, the Golden Gate Board of Directors voted to build a net system twenty feet below the bridge's platform that would catch and hold jumpers. The board then began working on raising the forty to fifty million dollars needed to install the nets. In the meantime, it's nothing but cold, hard water below.

Q Have children been raised by wolves?

A In a Moscow children's shelter, Ivan Mishukov was just another skinny, homeless kid. On the streets, however, he was leader of his pack. He roamed at will with this group, snatching food whenever hungry, huddling together at night in secret dens. Fiercely loyal to its leader, the pack had fought off the police three times when officers tried to seize Mishukov. Finally, in 1998, the police managed to wrest him from his followers and place him in a shelter where he would hopefully learn a better way life.

On the surface, this appears to be merely another sad story of juvenile crime. But in this case, Mishukov's pack was a literal one—a pack of dogs, not humans, and he was only six years old. He had been living with his canine family for two years. Although undernourished, he was otherwise healthy. Nor was he completely lacking in social skills. Once he got the hang of talking again, he told the staff how he and the dogs had shared food, warmth, and, most important, friendship.

Tales of feral, or "wolf," children reach far back into history. According to ancient mythology, Romulus and Remus, the founders of Rome, were suckled by a wolf. In 1800, Jean Itard, a French doctor, took in a mysterious boy he named Victor. Victor had been found wandering in the woods, unclothed and unkempt. His lack of speech and calloused feet led Itard to believe he had been living in the wild for quite some time. Itard's book about his attempt to civilize Victor, *The Wild Boy of Aveyron*, is considered a classic case study. What makes us human, he asks: nature or nurture? Was Victor raised by wolves, or was he simply an abused and possibly autistic child who had fled his family? Victor himself could never answer that question. He died at age forty without ever becoming fully articulate.

Closer to modern times, in 1920, two girls, Kamala (approximately eight years old) and Amala (eighteen months) were discovered in a wolves' den in southern India. Again, it never became clear how or why they got there. Other documented cases of feral children include ten-year-old Axel Rivas of Talcahuano, Chile, discovered living with a pack of dogs in 2001, and Angel, an abandoned Kenyan baby who was rescued by a dog and found sheltered among the dog's nursing pups in 2005. Rivas, too, reportedly received nourishment from a female dog, lending surprising credence to the old Roman legend.

Why are stories of feral children so compelling? In most instances, they reflect great poverty and hardship, yet they also remind us that "animal" is not the opposite of "human." Animals may nurture those driven to the margins of human society, and we may someday discover clues to the mysteries of nature from those who have truly taken a walk on the wild side.

Q Was there a real Sherlock Holmes?

A Since bursting onto the scene in 1887, Sherlock Holmes has become quite the celebrity. The members of his fan club, sometimes dubbed the Baker Street Irregulars, number in the hundreds of thousands worldwide. In the twentieth century, many readers were so convinced that Holmes was a real person that they sent mail to his address at 221b Baker Street in London. In the twenty-first century, he has his own page on Facebook.

Holmes is, of course, fictional. But is the detective based on fact? Author Sir Arthur Conan Doyle claimed that he modeled his famous detective on Dr. Joseph Bell (1837–1911) of the University of Edinburgh. Doyle had been Bell's assistant when Doyle was a medical student at the university from 1877 to 1881.

Like everyone else, Doyle was awed by Bell's ability to deduce all kinds of details regarding the geographical origins, life histories, and professions of his patients by his acute powers of observation. The doctor had what his students called "the look of eagles"; little escaped him. Reportedly, he could tell a working man's trade by the pattern of the calluses on his hands and what countries a sailor had visited by his tattoos.

In 1892 Doyle wrote an appreciative letter to his old mentor, saying, "It is most certainly to you that I owe Sherlock Holmes." The resemblance between Bell and Holmes was strong enough to impress Bell's fellow Scotsman Robert Louis Stevenson. After reading several Sherlock Holmes stories in a popular magazine, Stevenson sent a note to Doyle asking, "Can this be my old friend Joe Bell?"

When queried by journalists about the fictitious doppelganger, Bell modestly replied that "Dr. Conan Doyle has, by his imaginative genius, made a great deal out of very little, and his warm remembrance of one of his old teachers has coloured the picture." Nevertheless, Bell was pleased to write an introduction to the 1892 edition of *A Study in Scarlet,* the tale that had launched Holmes's career as a sleuth—and Doyle's as a writer. By the mid-1890s, Doyle had largely abandoned medicine for the life of a full-time writer.

Bell's association with Holmes wasn't his only claim to fame. He was a fellow of the Royal College of Surgeons of Edinburgh, the author of several medical textbooks, and one of the founders of modern forensic pathology. The University of Edinburgh honored his legacy by establishing the Joseph Bell Centre for Forensic Statistics and Legal Reasoning in March 2001.

One of the center's first initiatives was to develop a software program that could aid investigations into suspicious deaths. "It takes an overview of all the available evidence," said Jeroen Keppens, one of the program's developers, "and then speculates on what might have happened." Police detectives have praised the potential of the software, which is called, fittingly, Sherlock Holmes.

Q What's the most dangerous job in the world?

A Here's a quick experiment: Try to answer the question in your head first. We'll give you a while to mull it over. Come back when you think you've got the answer.

Done? Did you say something like a firefighter or a police officer? Working in the army? Well, while they're all dangerous, worthwhile jobs, none of these is the most dangerous job by a long shot. You're getting closer if you said miner, pilot, or even logger, but you're still not on the button.

The most dangerous job in the world is...a fisher. Yes, your favorite weekend pastime just became a whole lot more sinister. We're not talking Sundays spent lounging around on some peaceful lake, however; this is commercial fishing in rough, freezing ocean water. In 2006, 141.7 "fishers and related fishing workers" out of every 100,000 died, according to the Department of Labor's Bureau of Labor Statistics. That's compared to a rate of 87.8 out of every 100,000 aircraft pilots and flight engineers, who come in second place. Police officers and sheriff's officers (16.8 of 100,000) and firefighters (16.6 of 100,000) even trail farmers and ranchers (37.1 of 100,000) and roofers (33.9 of 100,000).

If there's one specific job in the fishing industry that you want to avoid, it's Alaskan crab fishing. These people fish in freezing waters, dragging up and unloading massive catches, and they also have to deal with storms. The crab-fishing season is extremely short, generally between October and January. The red king crab season used to be only three to five days but was recently expanded to three months. Either way, the fishers have to stay at sea for days at a time with very little rest in order to catch enough to meet their quotas. Their fatality rate is close to 300 out of every 100,000—not great odds.

And you thought a meeting in the conference room with your boss was a harrowing experience.

Q Where can you buy truth serum?

A Contrary to what your favorite action movies and espionage novels would have you believe, truth serum is not a drug that can be purchased just about anywhere. If you suspect your spouse of being unfaithful, for example, you can't hop on down to the local grocery and pick up a bottle over the counter. Even if you somehow convince a doctor to write a prescription for the serum, you'll have difficulty procuring it. This is probably for the best, as a dose of truth serum administered by inexperienced hands could be fatal.

Truth serum, more accurately known as sodium pentothal, is a highly potent barbiturate. It got its common name (truth serum) from its use in interrogations, particularly during the Cold War. The drug impairs higher brain function. The drugged individual becomes susceptible to suggestion, possessing a weakened power of will and an extremely limited ability to refuse any manner of request. Truth serum does not force a person to tell the truth—but it does make lying difficult, and it puts the individual into a state of mind in which he or she usually is going to take the easy way out.

Created in the 1930s by scientists working for Abbott Laboratories, the drug was used initially as anesthesia. It is still used in this way, especially in cases that require fast action—such as an emergency Caesarean section—though the drug is more commonly used by veterinarians. It has also been used to induce medical comas and, in larger doses, as a lethal injection.

Sodium pentothal is no longer administered in interrogations in the United States. The Supreme Court ruled in 1963 that all confessions given under the influence of the drug are inadmissible in court. This makes sense, considering the effect of sodium pentothal is akin to a magnified state of inebriation. A suspect might be less likely to construct a cogent lie, but this does not mean that he or she is telling the truth—those who are interrogated in this manner have problems keeping fact and fantasy separated.

Abbott Laboratories continues to produce the drug, marketing it as an anesthetic and not a truth serum. To purchase it in any quantity, you must be affiliated with a hospital or the correct branch of government. Or you need to be the protagonist in an espionage novel.

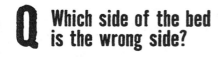 **Which side of the bed is the wrong side?**

A This is truly a question of critical importance, lest you spend every minute of every day in a funk. Those who get up on the wrong side of the bed, as we all know, are a blight on society, casting a pall on everyone who comes into their presence.

To help you avoid being the one under the rain clouds, we'll let you in on the secret: It's the left side. Do whatever you have to do in order to get up on the right side—pushing your bed against the wall works nicely—and you should be fine.

But what's wrong with the left side? If you were a Roman living around the time of Julius Caesar, you might ask, "What *isn't* wrong with the left side?"

The ancient Romans distrusted everything left: left-handedness, entering a house with the left foot forward, even setting the left foot down first when getting out of bed. If it could be done on the right side, with the right hand, or with the right foot, then that was the way it should be done.

There is an entire history of myths that associate evil with left-handedness. For instance, the devil is reputed to be left-handed, and it is with the left hand that he baptizes his followers. Or so they say. Also, according to the Satanic Bible, Satanists follow the "Left-Hand Path," which is the path opposite that of the Christian faith.

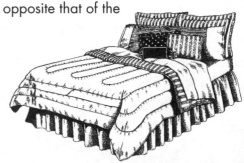

From the very beginning of recorded time, the left side has been distrusted. In fact, the Latin word for "left" *(sinistro)* is the root of the word "sinister." In almost all cultures, this belief has been held.

Left-handed people are no longer treated as devil worshippers, as they once were by practitioners of the Catholic faith. Sure, biases continue to exist—scissors, notebooks, and guitars all spring to mind—but lefties are treated as average human beings in most respects.

Still, just to be safe, remember to get up on the right side of the bed. That is to say, the correct side, which is also the right side. And just for good measure, you should probably let your right foot hit the floor first. Your day might be better for it.

Q Who determines which species are endangered?

A What do the Indiana bat, the San Francisco garter snake, and the Hawaiian dark-rumped petrel have in common? They all appeared on the first list of endangered species issued by the U.S. Fish and Wildlife Service (USFWS) in 1966. The list, compiled by nine biologists from the department's Committee on Rare and Endangered Wildlife Species, was at least in part the government's response to the furor sparked by Rachel Carson's 1962 book *Silent Spring,* which examined the impact of pesticides on the environment.

The Endangered Species Act of 1973 widened the scope of the USFWS's power, giving the federal government the authority to protect the habitats of endangered species from development, whether or not those habitats rested on public lands. Meanwhile, on a global level, the International Union for the Conservation of Nature (IUCN) had released its own list in 1962, the Red List of Threatened Species. Based on research conducted by the multinational Species Survival Commission, this list inspired the 1963 formation of the Convention on International Trade in Endangered Species of Wild Flora and Fauna.

By the end of the twentieth century, environmentalism had become a major movement and the phrase "endangered species" was part every school kid's vocabulary. But what does "endangered" mean? How many of a species have to die off before the remaining ones are considered endangered? Obviously, numbers alone don't tell the entire story. First, it can be hard to count individual members of a species in the wild. Second, it's difficult to compare the populations of small life-forms with those of larger ones. Ten thousand pomace flies can be just as endangered as ten polar bears, though hardly as photogenic.

The criteria used by the IUCN to determine whether a species is endangered include decrease in total population, decrease in the range of habitat, and probability of extinction. The population of the western lowland gorilla, for instance, has declined more than 60 percent since the 1980s due to poaching, disease, and the loss of portions of its habitat. This combination of misfortunes has placed the animal high in the IUCN's critically endangered category. Species with this designation have a 50 percent chance of becoming extinct within ten years or during three generations, whichever is longer, if a major effort is not made to preserve them.

As of 2007, the IUCN had listed 16,306 endangered species worldwide and another 41,415 as threatened though not yet endangered. The USFWS listed 448 animals and 598 plants as endangered in the United States. Together, these two organizations provide us with a fairly accurate assessment of which species are at the greatest risk of being lost forever.

As for our old friends the Indiana bat, the San Francisco garter snake, and the Hawaiian dark-rumped petrel? They're still hanging in there. Not yet out of danger—but thanks to the work of environmentalists, not extinct either.

Q Who is John Doe?

A There is no single John Doe from whom the rest have followed. The name is today what it has always been: a placeholder. John Doe is used when a person's name is unknown or when a person wishes to remain anonymous.

The name first appeared in legal proceedings known as actions of ejectment, which were common in England from the early thirteen hundreds until 1852 and also were used in the United States. In these proceedings, John Doe was a fictional name for the plaintiff; the name substituted for the defendant was the equally fictional Richard Roe.

An action of ejectment could be brought to the court by a person who had been thrown out of his own property by a trespasser or who had rented his property to a tenant who stopped paying rent and refused to leave. Either way, the person occupying the property had no right to be there, and the owner wanted him out.

Enter John Doe and Richard Roe. The property owner claimed

in court to have granted a lease to John Doe; John Doe, in turn, claimed to have been kept from using the property by Richard Roe. A letter was then sent to Richard Roe, urging him to appear in court. Because there wasn't a Richard Roe—at least not at that address—the real-life defendant came to the court to speak on his own behalf. The court allowed this, at which point the fictional lease became moot and the subject turned to the ownership of the land's title.

Is your head spinning yet? The process was overly complex, and it's anyone's guess why a person couldn't use his own name to argue property issues. England's Common Law Procedure Act, which was passed in 1852, did away with the action of ejectment and streamlined eviction proceedings. American law, however, continued the practice well into the twentieth century, using the same proxies for actual citizens.

Who came up with these names? It is likely that John and Richard were chosen because they were common English names. The origins of Doe and Roe are murkier. They might refer to deer: A doe is a female deer, and a roe is a type of deer native to Europe. Or they might have been chosen because one indicates deer and the other fish ("roe" can also refer to a mass of fish eggs), the thought process being that both deer and fish were commonly poached. Either way, the origins seem to be as anonymous as the names themselves.

Q Who is Tom, and why does he peep?

A The epithet "peeping Tom" has become synonymous with voyeurs—people who get sexual gratification from spying on others. According to legend, the first peeping Tom was a village tailor in the eleventh century who disobeyed the infamous Lady

Godiva, the woman who supposedly rode nude on horseback through the town of Coventry, England, in protest of her husband's tax laws.

The story goes that Godiva ordered the townspeople to shut themselves up in their houses so that they wouldn't catch a glimpse of her womanly virtues as she made her way through town. But poor Tom the tailor let his curiosity—or perhaps a baser instinct—get the best of him, and he looked out of his window when Godiva passed by. Depending on which account you read, Tom was either struck blind or killed on the spot.

The Godiva legend had circulated for a while before storytellers began to include the Peeping Tom character—the addition probably occurred sometime in the late seventeen hundreds. Around that time, the term made an appearance in Francis Grose's *Classical Dictionary for the Vulgar Tongue*, a book of slang that defined a peeping Tom as "a curious prying fellow." The records of the city of Coventry—which held a yearly parade to commemorate the Godiva legend—mention paint for the effigy of Peeping Tom the tailor in a list of items that were needed for the annual pageant.

Historians have a few theories about why Peeping Tom was added to the Godiva story. Some believe that the legend needed another layer of morality: Because he disobeyed his mistress, Tom was severely punished. He may also represent a migration of legends surrounding Roland, a well-known character in French medieval literature and a symbol of independence. Furthermore, Tom's presence may be tied to Godiva's pious Catholicism—Protestants may have created the Peeping Tom legend during the Reformation as an insult to the Catholic Church.

When visiting Coventry today, you can see statues of both Lady Godiva and Peeping Tom—sort of. A large metal-and-stone monument to Lady Godiva sits under a canopy near a shopping center. Across from her, in a marketplace window, is a painted wooden statue of a man with the phrase "Peeping Tom" written underneath. It's likely that the wooden figure originally represented Saint George and was salvaged from a nearby abbey after it was destroyed. But he does appear to be to be staring directly at the Godiva statue—and from the looks of it, he's enjoying his new home more than any musty old church.

Although it's unclear whether Peeping Tom really existed, his deed has become part of our culture. In many societies, voyeurism is a prosecutable sexual crime. However, modern peeping Toms are usually charged with misdemeanors and are ordered to pay fines. At most, they serve short jail terms, which is nothing compared to the fate of the original peeping Tom.

Q Who was the real McCoy?

A This question doesn't have a definitive answer, although that hasn't stopped people from trying to find one. The phrase itself is invoked whenever a question of authenticity is raised. Given several options, the one true selection is referred to as "the real McCoy," meaning it is the genuine article and you should accept no substitute. But who is this McCoy fellow, and what makes him so real?

One of the most believable accounts involves a boxer who was active around the turn of the twentieth century. Norman Selby, who boxed under the name "Kid McCoy," was a frequent source of imitation, and it's said that he adopted the phrase "the Real McCoy" to distinguish himself from the drove of impostors.

Another explanation states that a brand of Scottish whiskey used the phrase as part of an advertising campaign, starting in 1870. G. Mackay & Co. Ltd. referred to itself as "the real Mackay," which is, of course, an alternate spelling (and pronunciation) of the now-popular idiom.

And then there's a theory that originates in the United States' prohibition period of the 1920s and 1930s. During this time, bootleg alcohol was quite a profitable business for those who weren't afraid to take some risks. It was even more profitable for the bootleggers who watered down their booze.

One man, however, wouldn't compromise the quality of the liquor he sold—you guessed it, a fellow named McCoy. Bill McCoy. He earned a hardy reputation by sailing between Canada and the United States with contraband rum or whiskey on board. Shrewdly, McCoy dropped anchor in international waters (usually just outside Boston, New York City, or Philadelphia), where prohibition laws weren't in effect, and sold his wares legally to those who sailed out to him.

Although he might have made more money in the short term by watering down the booze he sold, McCoy was in it for the long haul and refused to taint his product. Therefore, the goods from his ship came to be known as "the real McCoy"—there was no diluted booze in McCoy's bottles.

So, who was the *real* McCoy? We may never know for sure. It appears there were several.

Q Why are people afraid of clowns?

A Got a case of coulrophobia? You're not alone. Experts estimate that as many as one in seven people suffer from an abnormal or exaggerated fear of clowns. The symptoms of this strangely common affliction range from nausea and sweating to irregular heartbeat, shortness of breath, and an overall feeling of impending doom. Is the sight of Ronald McDonald more chilling than your Chocolate Triple Thick Shake? There could be a few reasons why.

The most common explanation for coulrophobia is that the sufferer had a bad experience with a clown at a young and impressionable age. Maybe the clown at Billy Schuster's fifth birthday party shot you in the eye with a squirting flower, doused your head with confetti, or accidentally popped the balloon animal he was making for you. Some of the most silly or mundane things can be petrifying when you are young. And though the incident may be long forgotten, a bright orange wig or bulbous red nose might be enough to throw you back into the irrational fears that plagued your younger days.

Who could blame you? If television and movies have taught us anything, it's that clowns often are creatures of pure evil. There's the Joker, Batman's murderously insane archenemy; the shape-shifting Pennywise from Stephen King's *It*; the human-eating alien clowns in *Killer Klowns from Outer Space*; and a possessed toy clown that comes to life and beats the bejesus out of a young Robbie Freeling in Steven Spielberg's *Poltergeist*.

Real-life serial killer John Wayne Gacy didn't do much for the clown cause, either. Before authorities found the bodies of 27 boys and young men in his basement crawl space, Gacy was known as a charming, sociable guy who enjoyed performing at children's parties dressed up as Pogo the Clown or Patches the Clown. That ended when his crimes were discovered, but even on death row he still had an unwholesome interest in clowning—he took up oil painting, and clowns were his favorite subjects.

It's enough to give anyone the heebie-jeebies. But some experts say there's more to coulrophobia than traumatic childhood events or pop-culture portrayals. Scholar Joseph Durwin points out that since ancient times, clowns, fools, and jesters have been given permission to mock, criticize, or act deviantly and unexpectedly. This freedom to behave outside of normal social boundaries is exactly what makes clowns so threatening.

A *Nursing Standard* magazine interview of 250 people ages four to sixteen revealed that clowns are indeed "universally scary." Researcher Penny Curtis reported some kids found clowns to be "quite frightening and unknowable." Seems it has a lot to do with that permanent grease-painted grin. Because the face of a clown never changes, you don't know if he's relentlessly gleeful or about to bite your face off. In the words of Bart Simpson: "Can't sleep; clown will eat me."

Q Why do drive-up ATMs have Braille?

A Ever since Helen Keller first met Anne Sullivan in the late eighteen hundreds, visually impaired people have made tremendous strides in the United States. They can now easily use computers, read books, shop, and engage in a whole range of other activities that people associate with a normal life. Despite all of these advances, though, blind people still are unable to drive cars. Which leads to this obvious imponderable: Why is it necessary for drive-up automatic teller machines (ATMs) to have Braille pads?

There are a number of potential answers to this incongruous question. When one is dealing with sheer, unadulterated illogic, it is usually safe to look to the United States government first for a possible explanation. And sure enough, the government is behind the installation of Braille pads on drive-up ATMs.

In 1990, the government passed the American with Disabilities Act, a landmark bill that prohibits discrimination against disabled Americans. One need go no further than Section 4.34 of the act, which specifically details that ATMs be outfitted with a special apparatus for people with visual impairments, to find the answer to our question. The act requires that all ATMs be accessible to the blind; it does not make a distinction between drive-up and walk-up automated tellers, and as a result, all ATMs are equipped with Braille pads.

Economists will point out that once the government deemed Braille to be necessary on ATMs, it was a matter of efficiency for ATM producers to put the pad on all ATMs, whether they be drive-up or walk-up. Producing both Braille and non-Braille ATMs would require different molds, different inventories, and other logistical inefficiencies. And since the presence of Braille dots doesn't hurt anyone, why not put them on every ATM?

Besides, the Braille on those drive-through ATMs might come in handy. One can imagine situations in which a visually impaired person would need to use a drive-up ATM—when riding in a cab, for example. (Would you give your PIN to a cab driver?) Of course, this doesn't explain how the blind are able to use an ATM touch-screen—but that's another answer to another question.

Q What makes something "art"?

A If you want to see a name-calling, hair-pulling intellectual fight (and who doesn't?), just yell this question in a crowded coffee shop. After centuries of debate and goatee-stroking, it's still a hot-button issue.

Before the fourteenth century, the Western world grouped painting, sculpture, and architecture with decorative crafts such as pottery, weaving, and the like. During the Renaissance, Michelangelo and the gang elevated the artist to the level of the poet—a genius who was touched by divine inspiration. Now, with God as a collaborator, art had to be beautiful, which meant that artists had to recreate reality in a way that transcended earthly experience.

In the nineteenth and twentieth centuries, artists rejected these standards of beauty; they claimed that art didn't need to fit set requirements. This idea is now widely accepted, though people still disagree over what is and isn't art.

A common modern view is that art is anything that is created for its own aesthetic value—beautiful or not—rather than to serve some other function. So, according to this theory, defining art comes down to the creator's intention. If you build a chair to have something to sit on, the chair isn't a piece of art. But if you build an identical chair to express yourself, that chair *is* a piece of art. Marcel Duchamp demonstrated this in 1917, when he turned a urinal upside down and called it "Fountain." He was only interested in the object's aesthetic value. And just as simply as that: art.

This may seem arbitrary, but to the creator, there is a difference. If you build something for a specific purpose, you measure success by how well your creation serves that function. If you make pure art, your accomplishment is exclusively determined by how the creation makes you feel. Artists say that they follow their hearts, their muses, or God, depending on their beliefs. A craftsperson also follows a creative spirit, but his or her desire for artistic fulfillment is secondary to the obligation to make something that is functional.

Many objects involve both kinds of creativity. For example, a big-budget filmmaker follows his or her muse but generally bends to studio demands to try to make the movie profitable. (For instance, the movie might be trimmed to ninety minutes.) Unless the director has full creative control, the primary function of the film is to get people to buy tickets. There's nothing wrong with making money from your art, but purists say that financial concerns should never influence the true artist.

By a purist's definition, a book illustration isn't art, since its function is to support the text and please the client—even if the text is a work of art. The counter view is that the illustration is art, since the illustrator follows his or her creative instincts to create it; the illustrator is as much an artistic collaborator as the writer.

Obviously, it gets pretty murky. But until someone invents a handheld art detector, the question of what makes something art will continue to spark spirited arguments in coffee shops the world over.

Q Which one is spotted most frequently: the Loch Ness Monster, Bigfoot, or Elvis?

A The skeptical answer is easy: It's a three-way tie, with each nonexistent creature being spotted zero times. But what fun is that?

Just for the sake of argument, let's say that each of these paranormal freaks—the slimy eel cruising the depths of the loch in Scotland, the hairy ape roaming the woods of the Pacific Northwest, and the hunka hunka burnin' love haunting the fast-food drive-thrus of the South—does, in fact, exist. Which one makes the most public appearances?

The Loch Ness Monster definitely has time on its side. Sightings date back to the sixth century, when the beast allegedly attacked a monk named Columba who was trying to rescue a swimmer. (After his death, Columba became a saint, for reasons having nothing to do with his Nessie wrestling.) But appearances of the monster were infrequent until the twentieth century, when Nessie turned into something of a publicity hound. It started in 1934 when the London *Daily Mail* published a grainy photograph that purported to show the creature's head rising above the surface of the water. Ever since that first taste of mass media fame, the monster has been making fairly regular appearances, if we can believe the reports.

Bigfoot—or Sasquatch, to his friends—also has a long history under his belt. Even before the arrival of Europeans, he was glimpsed in the towering forests of the Northwest, in what is now northern California, Oregon, Washington, and British Columbia. A seemingly nonviolent bipedal fellow covered in thick fur, Bigfoot generally shows up in the woods and then skulks off once he realizes that he's been spotted. The Bigfoot phenomenon really took off in 1958, when giant footprints were found in a logging camp in Humboldt County, California. This seminal event in Bigfoot history was later tainted when the family of Ray Wallace, a logger who worked in that camp, revealed that Wallace had staged the whole thing. Nevertheless, this hoax didn't end Bigfoot mania—the legend lives on.

Elvis Presley, meanwhile, is a slightly less mythical creature than Bigfoot or Nessie. Evidence suggests that a man of that name did indeed walk the earth, consuming large quantities of fried peanut butter and banana sandwiches while producing a long series of hit songs and terrible movies. Since the reports of his death in 1977, Elvis has continued to live in the not-so-suspicious minds of many of his devoted followers. From Kalamazoo to Kansas City, astonished correspondents have told stories of seeing the King of Rock 'n' Roll pumping gas, buying groceries, or delivering pizzas.

A psychiatrist, Dr. Donald Hinton, said that he had secretly prescribed pain killers for Elvis during the 1990s; later, Hinton published a book that he claimed to have co-written with a man named "Jesse," whom he said was Elvis incognito. There's a reason you've never heard of this book, and it has nothing to do with any of the vast cover-up conspiracies.

And that's the problem with determining which one of these guys has the highest profile: Among the reports from the poor souls who honestly believe they've had encounters with them, you also find plenty of obvious fakes and pranks, arranged by people who are looking for publicity, money, or just a good laugh. It's impossible to tally the number of—for lack of a better word—"legitimate" sightings.

But we aren't afraid of a challenge, no matter how preposterous it is. We thought long and hard about this one and argued endlessly amongst ourselves in order to reach a consensus. So, our pick for the winner? Until either Nessie or Bigfoot plays a string of sold-out concerts in Las Vegas, we're backing the King.

Q Why does an orchestra conductor need a baton?

A So there was this seventeenth-century composer named Jean-Baptiste Lully who was conducting his beautiful music at a rehearsal. As always, he was keeping time with a huge wooden staff that he pounded on the floor. On this fateful day, however, Lully missed the floor and drove the staff right into his foot.

No, this is not the moment the conductor's baton was born. Lully did not have an epiphany and say, "You know, I should use something smaller to direct my music."

Nevertheless, the moment remains part of music history. An abscess developed on Lully's right foot that turned to gangrene. The composer did not have the foot amputated, causing the gangrene to spread and eventually leading to his death. There you have it—a conducting fatality!

So when did conductors trade in those clumsy, and potentially lethal, wooden staffs for the symbolically powerful batons? And do they really need them? Don't a conductor's hands contain ten God-made batons?

Some conductors today use their hands and fingers, but most have a baton that they move to the music. The feeling is that the baton—usually ten to twenty-four inches long and made of wood, fiberglass, or carbon—magnifies a conductor's patterns and gestures, making them clearer for the orchestra or ensemble.

Orchestras date to the late sixteenth century during the Baroque period, and conductors back then used the same type of staff that felled Lully. Sometimes there was no conductor at all. Instead, the leader was most often a keyboardist, who would guide the orchestra when his hands were free, or a violinist, who would set the tempo and give directions by beating the neck of his instrument or making other movements. At other times, the keyboardist or violinist simply played louder so the rest of the orchestra could follow his lead.

As written music grew more complex, orchestras needed more direction than a keyboardist or violinist could provide. Conductors started appearing in France in the eighteenth century and emerged in earnest early in the nineteenth century. Still, there was no baton—rolled up paper was the tool of choice.

German composer, violinist, and conductor Louis Spohr claimed to have introduced the formal baton to the music world in a performance in 1820, but that simply might have been boastfulness. It is widely thought that he only used a baton in rehearsals.

It's possible that German composer, pianist, and conductor Felix Mendelssohn was the first to use an actual baton in a performance. According to *The Cambridge Companion to Conducting,*

Mendelssohn used a baton in 1829 and again in 1832 with the Philharmonic Society of London. The next year, a baton was used regularly with the Philharmonic—and today, almost every conductor wields one.

Even though the baton is a lot safer than the wooden staff, there have been some accidents along the way. For example, German conductor Daniel Turk's motions became so animated during a performance in 1810 that he hit a chandelier above his head and was showered with glass. What is it with these guys?

There was more baton craziness in 2006 and 2007. First, the conductor of the Harvard University band set a record by using a baton that was ten and one-half or twelve and one-half feet long, depending on whom you listen to. The next year, the University of Pennsylvania band claimed to have bested that record with its fifteen-foot, nine-inch baton. There were no reports of a Lully moment on either occasion.

Q Why do speedometers list speeds faster than you can legally drive?

A Zip along a stretch of rural Texas Interstate at 80 miles per hour and you'll be driving just about as fast as you can go anywhere in our speed-craving country without risking a ticket. But unless you're driving some kind of Yugoslavian relic, you'll still have plenty of room to inch that needle higher on your car's speedometer. Let's say your ride is a 505-horsepower Chevrolet Corvette Z06—you'll have a whopping 120 miles per hour of speed-gauge breathing room. Is Chevy begging us to break the law? Is the company all but telling us to slam the gas pedal to the floor?

Ask experts why automakers install speedometers that mock posted limits—which usually range from 65 to 80 miles per hour on the highway, depending on the state you're in—and you will get discussions of manufacturing efficiencies, hints of subliminal messages, and psychological explanations that offer something in between.

"It's a one-word answer: testosterone," says Alex Fedorak, a veteran of more than two decades in car-company public relations. "It's a guy thing. They want to think they can do it, even if they never do."

Less sanguine is Richard Retting, senior transportation engineer with the Insurance Institute for Highway Safety, an underwriter-industry lobbying group. "There's no reason for any car to have a speedometer that goes over 80 miles per hour because there's no place in this country you can legally drive faster than that," Retting says. "Why car speedometers go up to 120 or 140 miles per hour makes no sense—except for marketing. It's no secret that speed is a key strategy for marketing vehicles in this country. Someone who bought a high-horsepower, high-speed car presumably would not be happy with a speedometer that gave the impression the car would not go up to that speed, even if they never approached that speed."

Automakers cite the economic efficiency of producing a single speedometer that's good in several countries, in which speed limits may be higher or in kilometers per hour. General Motors, which builds cars for use in virtually every nation on Earth, requires its speedometers to indicate true vehicle speed at all times and to reflect the top speed of the fastest-rated tire that can be used on a particular vehicle.

Betwixt talk of testosterone and tires lies the nuanced approach of Stuart Norris, who is responsible for GM's global instrument design strategies, Norris acknowledges issues of engineering and standardization, but he also waxes about speedometer aesthetics, about the way the numerals are distributed on the speedometer's face, and how large, elegant type sends one message (luxury) and starker, closely spaced markings another (sporty). And all this time, we thought a speedometer simply indicated how fast you were going. Who knew there's much more to it than that?

A speedometer that ended at, say, 85 miles per hour, would "look under-populated, half-baked, even childlike," Norris says. "There's a premium-ness associated with a more populated gauge." As for that final numeral, "On a vehicle that's rated for 155 miles per hour, we expect the gauge to indicate the capability of the vehicle, even though we don't expect the customer to drive that speed."

In the end, it's all about ego. A speedometer that goes up to 200 miles per hour connotes power, even if you can never fully unleash that power.

HISTORY'S MYSTERIES

Q Why is the bald eagle the U.S. national bird?

A After the U.S. founding fathers kicked the Brits out and hung up the "Under New Management" sign, they needed a few essential accessories: a system of government to run the joint, a flag to identify its ships, and a Great Seal for authenticating international treaties and agreements. Oddly enough, the Great Seal turned out to be a tricky one: Jefferson, Franklin, Adams, and the gang started spit-balling ideas on July 4, 1776. During the next six years, three different committees pitched designs, but Congress rejected all of them. In 1782, Congress gave the three unsatisfactory proposals to the Secretary of the Continental Congress, Charles Thomson, and asked him to take a crack at it.

Thomson liked certain elements from each of the earlier attempts, including a small white eagle from the third committee. As a history and classics buff, he knew that eagles had a long history as national emblems. Roman soldiers carried eagle-topped staffs into battle; medieval knights slapped them on their family coats of arms; and Germany, Russia, and Poland adopted them as national symbols. But while he liked the iconic nobility and strength of the eagle, Thomson thought it was important that the U.S. symbol be something unique to America, to underscore the young nation's independence from Europe. So he changed the bird to the bald eagle, which is indigenous to North America. (Incidentally, "bald" doesn't have anything to do with hair loss in this case—the term dates back to the thirteenth century and describes white coloration on the head.)

After less than a week of brainstorming, Thomson gave his ideas to one of the more artistically inclined members of the earlier committees, who produced a polished drawing of the design. Exactly one week after being tasked with the Seal design, Thomson presented these drawings to the Continental Congress, along with his own written description of the Great Seal (called a blazon), with the bald eagle as the central figure. Congress approved the design the same day, and the Great Seal was a hit. Before long, the eagle took off as a national symbol, and it was everywhere: money, buildings, novelty butter churns—the works.

Not everyone was a fan, however. In a 1784 letter to his daughter, Benjamin Franklin dissed the bald eagle as "a bird of bad moral character," because of its habit of stealing fish from the fishing hawk. He suggested that the turkey would make a better choice, noting, "The turkey is in comparison a much more respectable bird … he is besides (though a little vain and silly, it is true, but not the worse emblem for that) a bird of courage, and would not hesitate to attack a grenadier of the British guards, who should presume to invade his farm yard with a red coat on."

Franklin wasn't entirely serious, of course, but who knows? If he had pitched the idea a few years earlier, we might be known as the fightin' turkeys.

Q Couldn't the Irish have found something to eat besides potatoes to avoid famine?

A More than a million people starved to death in Ireland from 1845 to 1851. The disaster is called the Great Famine, but it wasn't really a famine. Only one crop failed: the potato. How could this have killed so many? Why didn't the Irish eat cabbage or scones or even chalupas, for crying out loud?

The answer is simple: Those who starved were poor. For generations, the impoverished in Ireland had survived by planting potatoes to feed their families. They had nothing else. Ireland's wealthy landowners grew a wide variety of crops, but these were shipped away and sold for profit. Most of the rich folks didn't care that the poor starved.

How did things get so bad? Irish History 101: The Catholics and the Protestants didn't like each other, and neither did the English and the Irish. Back then, the wealthy landowners were mostly Protestants from England, while the poor were Catholic peasants. The Irish peasants grew their food on small parcels of land that were rented from the hated English.

In the sixteenth century, a hitherto unknown item crossed the Atlantic from Peru, originally arriving in England and finally getting to Ireland in 1590: the potato. Spuds grew well in Ireland, even on the rocky, uneven plots that were often rented by peasants,  and they quickly became the peasants' main food source. Potatoes required little labor to grow, and an acre could yield twelve tons of them—enough to feed a family of six for the entire year, with leftovers for the animals.

We think of potatoes as a fattening food, but they're loaded with vitamins, carbohydrates, and even some protein. Add a little fish and buttermilk to the diet, and a family could live quite happily on potatoes. Potatoes for breakfast, lunch, and dinner might sound monotonous, but it fueled a population boom in Ireland. By the nineteenth century, three million people were living on the potato diet.

In 1845, though, the fungus *Phytophthora infestans,* or "late blight," turned Ireland's potatoes into black, smelly, inedible lumps. Impoverished families had no options, no Plan B. Their pitiful savings were wiped out, and they fled to the work houses—the only places where they could get food and shelter in return for their labor.

When the potato crop failed again the next year, and every year through 1849, people began dying in earnest—not just from starvation, but from scurvy and gangrene (caused by a lack of vitamin C), typhus, dysentery, typhoid fever, and heart failure. Overwhelmed and underfunded, the work houses closed their doors. Many people who were weakened by hunger died of exposure after being evicted from their homes. To top the disaster off, a cholera epidemic spread during the last year of the blight, killing thousands more.

The exact number of those who perished is unknown, but it's believed to be between one and two million. In addition, at least a million people left the country, and many of these wayward souls died at sea. All during that terrible time, plenty of food existed in Ireland, but it was consumed by the wealthy. The poor, meanwhile, had nothing. They were left to starve.

Q Did any congressmen vote against entering WWII?

A Only one—a congresswoman, actually. After Japan bombed Pearl Harbor on December 7, 1941, the American people were just about as unified as Americans get. Before the attack, the nation had been divided over whether to enter the war. But as soon as news of the bombing spread, the determination to act was overwhelming. President Franklin Delano Roosevelt delivered a rousing speech to a joint session of Congress, requesting a declaration of war. The Senate immediately voted for the resolution, 82 to 0. In the House of Representatives, 388 people voted for the resolution, 41 did not vote, and 1 voted against it.

The sole dissenting voice was Jeanette Rankin, a sixty-one-year-old pacifist Republican representative from Montana. When her name was called, she said, "As a woman, I can't go to war, and I refuse to send anyone else." Her words spurred loud booing from her fellow representatives. When Germany and Italy declared war against the United States on December 11, Congress voted unanimously to go to war against the two nations. In this case, Rankin voted present instead of no.

No one should have been surprised by Rankin's original no vote, given her background. She had made history in 1917 when she became the first woman in Congress; at the time, most states hadn't even given women the right to vote. However, her political career hit rough waters almost immediately. Her first vote came just four days after she took office, when President Woodrow Wilson asked Congress to approve his declaration of war against Germany.

Rankin was one of fifty representatives to vote against the resolution, but the press singled her out—many used her stance as an argument against women's suffrage. Congressional redistricting in Montana kept Rankin from running for re-election, so she ran for the Senate instead. She lost, due in part to her opposition to the war.

For the next two decades, Rankin stayed in the political arena as a lobbyist, pushing for better health care for children, among other causes. Then in 1940 she won one of Montana's congressional seats again after campaigning on an anti-war platform. But the tides shifted with Pearl Harbor, and her no vote effectively ended her career in public office. On her way back to her office after the vote, she even had to hide out in a phone booth to escape an angry mob.

Rankin stayed active in public policy over the years, however. And in 1968, at the age of 87, she led more than five thousand women, who called themselves "the Jeanette Rankin Brigade," in a march on Washington to protest the war in Vietnam. Given all of the political flip-flopping of today, you at least have to admire her consistency.

Q How did Europe divvy up the New World?

A Initially, it was really quite simple: The pope decided who got what. In 1493—one year after Christopher Columbus's first voyage—the largely Catholic kingdoms of Spain and Portugal were the only European players in the New World. Other countries were decades away from investigating the strange land; the Pilgrims wouldn't arrive at Plymouth Rock for more than a century.

Ferdinand and Isabella of Spain had financed Columbus's voyage and figured that they had an obvious claim to the lands he had discovered. But Portugal's King John II disagreed. He cited the fourteen-year-old Treaty of Alcaçovas, drafted when Portugal was exploring the coast of Africa. The treaty, which Spain had signed, gave Portugal all lands south of the Canary Islands. The New World was south of the Canaries, so it belonged to Portugal. Columbus, according to John, was trespassing on its land.

Isabella and Ferdinand of Spain were indignant. They brought up a law that dated back to the Crusades that said Christian rulers could seize control of any heathen land in order to spread the Catholic faith. *So there.* Rather than go to war, they asked the pope to resolve the issue because, frankly, Portugal had a big, powerful navy and Spain did not. (No one bothered to ask the native people in the New World what they had to say about this, in case you're wondering.)

Pope Alexander VI, of the infamous Borgia family, drew a line from the North Pole to the South, one hundred leagues west of the Cape Verde Islands, which was the site of a Portuguese colony. Portugal received every heathen land east of that line: the Azores, the Canary Islands, Africa (including Madagascar), and Saudi Arabia. Years later, explorers found that the north-south line went right through South America; this gave Portugal a chunk of that continent as well. That's why most Brazilians speak Portuguese to this day.

Spain got everything to the west of the pope's line. In 1494, when the treaty was signed at Tordesillas, no one realized that two huge continents sat in Spain's portion. Isabella and Ferdinand thought that they were getting only the puny Caribbean islands that Columbus had spotted. In fact, they were pissed off and felt cheated, but the pope's decision was final.

At least for a while. A later treaty changed the line, and then the British, French, Russians, and Dutch got in on the action and began claiming parts of the New World for themselves. The Treaty of Tordesillas was forgotten.

Q How many Germans were actually Nazis?

A The Nazis, or National Socialist German Workers' Party, ruled Germany with an iron fist from 1933 to 1945, but they never actually achieved official majority support from the German people, either in the form of votes or party membership.

Adolf Hitler became the Nazi Party chairman in 1921, but the German government banned the party in 1923 after a failed Nazi coup attempt. Hitler reconstituted the party in 1925 and, over the course of five years, built it from a peripheral splinter group into one of the leading conservative political parties in Germany. However, it still didn't have enough support to win a majority of votes in any election. In April 1932, Hitler garnered a mere 36.8 percent of the vote in his bid to become the leader of Germany, losing out to the incumbent, Paul von Hindenburg. That same year in July, however, the Nazis received 37.8 percent of the vote in parliamentary elections, the most among Germany's parties.

The second-biggest party, the Social Democrats, was threatened by the Nazi Party's rise. In an attempt to build a coalition government between the two parties (united against the communists), Hindenburg appointed Hitler as the new chancellor (head of the government) on January 30, 1933. At that point, there were about

1.4 million card-carrying Nazi Party members, which was less than 3 percent of the German population.

The Social Democrats hoped to control Hitler more effectively by giving him nominal power. But as chancellor, Hitler got the foothold he needed to turn Germany into a totalitarian dictatorship. Hindenburg called for new parliamentary elections in March 1933, and the Nazis turned up their intimidation tactics to sway voters away from the opposition. But even after fighting dirty, the Nazis won only 43.9 percent of the vote. The following July, Hitler declared the Nazi Party the sole political party of Germany, effectively ending democratic rule.

Even under totalitarian oppression, most Germans never joined the Nazi Party. Hitler made membership mandatory for only higher-level civil servants and bureaucrats. In fact, from May 1933 to May 1939, party membership was, for the most part, closed— Hitler wanted the Nazis to include a select elite rather than the entire German population. According to the Nazi Party's official *Zentralkartei* (master file), there were 7.2 million Nazi Party members between its reconstitution in 1925 and its dissolution in May 1945, the vast majority of whom joined after Hitler came to power. Based on these numbers, only around 10 percent of Germany's citizens were card-carrying Nazis.

If you define Nazis more broadly, as people who believed in the party's cause, it's impossible to determine the actual number. After Germany's crushing defeat in World War II, people weren't exactly clamoring to confess their past Nazi loyalties.

Q How terrible was Ivan the Terrible?

A About as cruel and terrible as anyone could be. It's pretty hard to whitewash the reputation of a man who murdered friends, tortured enemies, and beat his own son to death.

Ivan IV became ruler of Russia in 1533 at the tender age of three, after his father died. His mother was a regent; her family and other nobles—called *boyars*—fought each other often and violently for control of the government. Ivan grew to hate them. His tutors were monks, and he learned an intolerant brand of Christianity that stayed with him his whole life.

In 1547, while still a teenager, Ivan had himself crowned the first tsar—a word meaning "God's anointed." That's how he thought of himself. He made pilgrimages, built churches, and fancied himself chosen by God to hold absolute power—including the power to torture or kill anyone who disagreed with him.

In the early part of his reign, Ivan was not a bad ruler. He called consultative assemblies, issued a new law code, reformed local governments, and conquered some Tatar states. His first marriage was happy and lasted more than twelve years. But when his first wife died—he was married seven times—Ivan started behaving like a sadistic lunatic and earned his nickname, "The Terrible."

Convinced that his beloved wife had been poisoned by the hated *boyars,* Ivan attacked the people of that class by seizing their lands and executing them whenever he decided they were traitors. He also turned on old friends and advisors and had the highest-ranking church official in Moscow murdered. His most shocking crime was the murder of his own son and heir, Ivan, in 1581. He beat his adult son in front of the man's wife, then delivered the death blow with an iron-pointed staff.

Ivan held power longer than any other Russian ruler. After Ivan died in 1584, his feeble-minded son, Feodor, took over because he was the last remaining heir. An autopsy done centuries after his death revealed that Ivan's spine had been fused by disease, probably causing intense pain, which experts say may explain part of his insane behavior. But only part.

Q Was math discovered or invented?

A This question has been kicked around by just about every serious philosopher over the past 2,500 years or so. In that light, it might seem somewhat curious to find it discussed in the same book that brings you questions like "Who invented the smiley face?" But, hey, we're not afraid to tackle the tough ones.

Invented things didn't exist before they were invented. They may meet a pressing, timeless human need—such as, you know, the electric foot-callus sander—but they weren't around until a lightbulb went off in someone's head.

Discovered things always have existed, such as the element strontium. It's been around forever, but nobody knew it until 1787 when Scottish miners near the village of Strontian found it in the mineral strontianite.

Where does math fit in? To many folks, math is simply a symbolic representation of the real, physical world. You can call the number two "two" or you can call it "Shirley," but the concept under-lying 2 + 2 = 4 has always been there. When man figured out that concept, he discovered math. This is what Plato felt.

But others question this belief on fairly abstract philosophical grounds, essentially saying that if math "existed" before we conceived of it or discovered it, then we have to accept the existence of an abstract notion even without human brains there to be aware of it. Philosophers call this "theism," and apparently it makes some of them nervous.

To us, it makes sense that math was discovered. Math is a specific, precise, rigorous way of describing the physical world, involving hard-and-fast rules. There are different ways of expressing or arriving at the concept of "four," but that concept is always distinct from "five" in precisely the same way; you can't say that four things are five things. This reality was there as soon as there were four things in the universe, even though people weren't around to understand it.

We're getting into metaphysics here—"If a tree falls in the forest..." stuff—but that's the way philosophy is. Makes your high school geometry seem pretty straightforward in comparison, doesn't it?

Q Were the *Mayflower* Pilgrims as straightlaced as we learned in school?

A They tried to be. But you know how it goes: A shoe gets unbuckled, a bonnet comes loose, and suddenly your hormones go into overdrive. The next thing you know, your horn o' plenty hath spilleth forth with wicked abundance.

Our modern-day image of the stern, clean-living, God-fearing residents of Plymouth Colony is largely mythical. It's an illusion that took shape during the nineteenth century, as some overzealous Americans attempted to construct an official, more respectable history of their burgeoning nation.

Historians can't even say for certain how many of the approximately one hundred passengers on the *Mayflower* in 1620 were Puritans and how many were just trying to find better lives away from the grueling poverty that gripped England at the time; it's generally believed that there were more of the latter than the former. And they didn't call themselves "Pilgrims"—they were known to have referred to themselves as "Old Planters" and "Old Comers." Draw your own conclusions from that.

While we don't have many racy details about their private lives, we do know that by 1636, the colonists had a published set of laws that listed capital offenses; among them were sodomy, rape, buggery, and some cases of adultery. So they were certainly obsessed with sex, if not necessarily always having it.

Court records from the colony indicate that sex-related crimes were common transgressions. Fornication, which was defined as having sex outside of marriage, was a frequently committed crime, one that often resulted in a fine. Sometimes, the evidence for a conviction consisted solely of the birth of a child in the early months of a marriage.

The only recorded execution for a sex crime occurred in 1642, when seventeen-year-old Thomas Granger was convicted of buggery. The young man had engaged in unfortunate amorous relationships with sheep, and he paid the ultimate price for it.

Less severe penalties (relatively speaking) often consisted of whippings. (Although it must be said that we can think of certain personality types who might choose a life of crime because of that sort of "punishment.") And like what happened to Hester Prynne in Nathaniel Hawthorne's *The Scarlet Letter,* adulterers were sometimes required to wear the capital letters AD on their clothing.

No, the Pilgrims were not exactly saints. But they certainly took their sins seriously.

Q What did Custer stand for in his last stand?

A Gold and his own ego, mostly. Custer's Last Stand (a.k.a. the Battle of Little Bighorn) was the culmination of years of hostility between the United States government and the Sioux Indian tribe. In the 1860s, the U.S. Army battled Sioux and other tribes in the Dakota and Wyoming territories for control of the Bozeman Trail, a path that passed through Sioux buffalo-hunting grounds to gold mines in Montana. The government abandoned the effort in 1868 and negotiated the Fort Laramie Treaty, which gave the Sioux, Cheyenne, and Arapaho tribes ownership of much of what is now South Dakota.

Then in 1874, Lieutenant Colonel George Armstrong Custer led an expedition to the area to find a suitable location for an army post and investigate rumors of gold. He verified that there was gold in the Black Hills, on Indian land. The government tried to buy back the land, but renegade Sioux Indians who refused to abide by U.S.

regulations blocked the sale. The government issued an ultimatum that all Sioux warriors and hunters report to reservation agency outposts by a certain date; failure to comply would be viewed as an act of hostility.

When the renegade Sioux warriors ignored the order, the army mounted a campaign to round them up and force them into designated areas on the Indian reservation. Brigadier General Alfred Terry led the campaign, and Custer commanded one of the regiments, the Seventh Cavalry. Terry ordered Custer to lead his regiment to the south of the presumed Sioux location and wait until Terry positioned the rest of the soldiers to the north; this way, they could advance simultaneously from both sides.

But on June 25, 1876, Custer came across a Sioux village in the Valley of Little Bighorn and decided to attack it by himself. Against the advice of his officers, he divided his regiment into three groups: one to scout the bluffs overlooking the valley; one to start the attack on the upper end of the village; and one—made up of 210 men, including Custer—to attack from the lower end of the village.

Bad plan. As many as three thousand Sioux and Cheyenne men (many more than Custer had expected) forced the first group of soldiers into retreat, and then they turned their full attention to Custer and his men, killing every last one in less than an hour. News reports right after the incident said that Custer's actions were the result of foolish pride. But before long, he had morphed into a heroic figure, one who fueled outrage against the Indians in the West.

Drawings and paintings depicting the battle, usually titled "Custer's Last Fight" or "Custer's Last Stand," kept the battle fresh in people's minds for decades to follow. "Stand," in the military terminology of the day, meant simply the act of opposing an enemy rather than retreating or yielding. Custer definitely stood for that, if nothing else.

Q What was the Rape of Nanking?

A This menacing phrase refers to the brutal mass murders, arson, rapes, and pillaging that took place in Nanking (now called Nanjing), China, from December 1937 to February 1938. The victims were mostly Chinese, both civilians and soldiers, and the aggressors were the invading Japanese army. Between two hundred and fifty thousand and three hundred thousand people were killed.

Here's the background: Japan invaded and occupied Manchuria, in northeastern China, in 1931. Meeting no real opposition, Japan renamed the province Manchukuo and made plans to expand Japanese power in Asia. At the time, a worldwide economic depression preoccupied many countries (including the United States), and fascist dictatorships were on the rise in Europe.

Air raids over Nanking began in the brutally hot summer of 1937. By November, Japan announced that a million soldiers had landed and were marching on Nanking, which was the capital of the Republic of China and a major port on the Yangtze River.

The claim may have been true—there might actually have been a million soldiers. But they were deployed without much food, so looting was encouraged by their officers. Predictably, turning military men loose to pillage led to wanton violence and murders. In addition, the Chinese army surrendered in huge numbers, and the Japanese weren't prepared to keep them captive. It was easier to shoot them than to build prisons for them; in fact, the official Japanese orders were to "take no prisoners."

Rapes and massacres took place before the city of Nanking fell in mid-December. Survivors told of seeing their homes burned and their families—even children—gunned down. Girls were gang-raped and killed.

The Japanese started a campaign of absolute terror against the Chinese. Innocent people were mowed down by machine guns as they tried to flee the city, and so were the soldiers who surrendered. Mass murders—not of hundreds of people but of *thousands*—became common. In one case, both survivors and Japanese soldiers told of the killing of up to twenty thousand Chinese troops in one day. Other diaries and interviews described grenades being thrown into crowds, poison gas clouds, and rows and rows of civilians being bayoneted.

Soon, mountains of bodies lined the roads. The carcasses clogged the waterways, as well; one soldier called the Yangtze a "river of corpses." A destroyed bridge near Nanking's Shuixi Gate was replaced by bodies that were thrown into the river until they were piled so high that they formed a new bridge. Doors and planks were arranged on top so that the "bridge" could be crossed.

By February 1938, gangs of laborers were burying or burning the bodies, and the worst of the bloodshed was over. Today, the Rape of Nanking stands out as a black mark on the history of humankind.

Q What was World War I called before World War II?

A We certainly don't name wars like we used to. Once, we had poetry in our conflicts. We had the Pastry War, the War of the Roses, and the War of the Oranges. We had the War of the Three Sanchos, the War of the Three Henries, and the War of the Eight Saints. We even had something called the War of Jenkins' Ear.

As the twentieth century rolled around, this convention of applying sweet nicknames to war—and everything else—was still going strong. Ty Cobb was given the moniker "The Georgia Peach." And the 1904 World's Fair was not-so-humbly called "The Greatest of Expositions." It was an optimistic time. Advances in medicine were helping people live longer and Henry Ford's mass production of the automobile made the world seem smaller than ever.

This combination of optimism and the tradition of poetic nicknames led to some understandable debate in 1914, when an assassin's bullet felled the Archduke Franz Ferdinand and launched all of Europe—and much of the world—into all-out war. For the next few years, Germans rampaged through the continent, looking rather silly in spiked hats; mustard gas (which was not nearly as delicious as it sounded) crippled and killed countless men and women; and all across Europe, an entire generation was slowly wiped out.

What to name this gruesome conflict? The journalists and historians went to work. A number of possibilities were discarded, including "The German War" and "The War of the Nations," before two names were settled upon, which are still used today in conjunction with

World War I: "The Great War," which retains a simplistic elegance, and, more popularly, "The War to End All Wars."

Melodramatic? Yes. Full of hubris? Definitely. Remember, though, these were the same people who famously labeled the Titanic "unsinkable."

No, we don't name wars like we used to. But even if the stylistic flourishes of yore have mostly disappeared, it is comforting to know that we're still not above a little hubris and melodrama. Anyone remember "Mission Accomplished"?

Q Who invented the guillotine?

A One of the great ironies in history is that Dr. Joseph-Ignace Guillotin was an opponent of capital punishment. But despite the fact that he was the guillotine's namesake, he did not invent the device. The infamous death machine's true creators were Antoine Louis, the French doctor who drew up the initial design around 1792, and Tobias Schmidt, the German piano maker, who executed it. (Pun intended.)

Guillotin's contribution came a bit earlier. As a delegate to France's National Assembly of 1789, he proposed the novel idea that if executions could not be banned entirely, the condemned should at least be entitled to a swift and relatively merciful death. What's more, he argued that all criminals, regardless of whether they were rich or poor, should be executed by the same method.

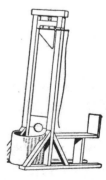

This last point may seem obvious, but prior to the French Revolution, wealthy miscreants who were up to be offed could slip the executioner a few coins to guarantee a speedy dispatch. Poorer ones often went "coach class"—they got to be the coach while horses tied to their arms and legs pulled them in four different directions. What a way to go!

In April 1792, the Assembly used its new guillotine for the first time on a platform in Paris' Place de Grève. Two vertical wooden beams served as runners for the slanted steel blade and stood about fifteen feet high. At the bottom, two boards with a round hole, called the *lunette,* locked the victim's head in place. The blade was hoisted to the top with pulleys and released with a lever. After a few grisly mishaps, executioners learned to grease the grooves on the beams with tallow in order to ensure that no one was left with half a head, which in this case was definitely not better than having none at all.

The first head to roll was that of Nicolas Jacques-Pelletier, a common thief. During the Reign of Terror, from January 1793 to July 1794, more than ten thousand people had an exit interview with "Madame Guillotine," including King Louis XVI and his wife, Marie Antoinette. The daily parade of victims drew crowds of gawkers. Journalists printed programs, vendors sold refreshments, and nearby merchants rented out seats with unobstructed views. This bloody period ended with the execution of Robespierre, one of the Revolution's leaders and an early advocate of the guillotine.

France continued to use the guillotine in cases of capital punishment throughout the nineteenth and twentieth centuries. The last official guillotine execution took place on September 10, 1977.

Because they were embarrassed by their association with this instrument of terror, the descendants of Joseph Guillotin petitioned the government to change the name of the machine. The government declined to comply, so the family changed its name instead and passed into obscurity. Not so for the guillotine itself: Though it is now relegated to museums, it remains a grim symbol of power, punishment, and sudden death.

Q Who shot whom in the O.K. Corral?

A First, the famous showdown in Tombstone, Arizona, didn't take place in the O.K. Corral. It happened in the city's vacant lot No. 2. Somehow, "The Shoot-Out in Vacant Lot No. 2" doesn't have quite the same ring to it, so a savvy journalist or scriptwriter must have moved the action a few yards over.

Second, despite what the movies may suggest, it wasn't a simple tale of white hats versus black hats. The real story has as many twists and turns as a warren of prairie dog tunnels, with a roundup of suspects that includes carousing cowboys, contentious lawmen, corrupt politicians, card sharks, cattle rustlers, a dentist named Doc, and Doc's lady friend (the appropriately named Big Nose Kate).

What do we know for sure? On October 26, 1881, at around 3:00 P.M., four men entered the lot behind the O.K. Corral: Wyatt Earp; his brothers, Virgil and Morgan; and John Henry "Doc" Holliday. There, they encountered Ike Clanton, his brother Billy, Frank and Tom McLaury, and Billy Claiborne. Thirty seconds later, both of the McLaury brothers and Billy Clanton were dead. Virgil and Morgan Earp sustained serious wounds, Holliday suffered a minor injury, and Wyatt walked out without a scratch.

What brought them there? Trouble had been brewing between the Earp and Clanton factions for some time. Doc Holliday, a Philadelphia-trained dentist, preferred playing cards to pulling teeth, and this habit often left him short of cash. Earlier in 1881, he had been accused of stagecoach robbery by his own girlfriend, Big Nose Kate. The Earp brothers suspected that Ike Clanton had put her up to it to deflect suspicion from his own friends. When four of those friends turned up dead, Clanton accused the Earps, and the bad blood began to boil.

Who fired first? Most historians agree that Holliday and Morgan Earp started it, one wounding Frank McLaury and the other Billy Clanton. With that, as the locals say, "the ball had begun." An estimated thirty shots were fired within half a minute. Wyatt claimed that seventeen were his, though he is only thought to have killed one man, Tom McLaury.

The Earps and Holliday were ultimately acquitted of any wrongdoing. Several months later, Morgan Earp was shot to death by unknown assailants. Wyatt spent the next two years tracking down anyone he thought was connected with his brother's death. Was he "brave, courageous, and bold," as the song says? Or was he just a ruthless vigilante? The jury is still out. One thing is certain, though: Wyatt Earp was an American original, and his story will be told for generations to come.

Q Who took care of the aged and poor before Social Security and welfare programs?

A Just about everyone—except the government. For centuries, up to the Great Depression of the 1930s, families traditionally took care of grandparents and aging parents. Imagine Nana and

Poppa sharing your kitchen, your outhouse, your fireplace, and maybe even your bedroom. Now you know why people in those nineteenth-century daguerreotypes never smiled.

Few people had health insurance, so if someone lost a job or broke a leg, family members were expected to provide support. If that wasn't enough to keep bread on the table, churches, fraternal clubs, and lodges had special funds to aid families in need. The Red Cross and other organizations like it also stood ready to help. In big cities, where immigrant populations were high, aid societies for different ethnic groups sprang up to offer loans, employment, and even shelter during tough periods.

The system worked fairly well for a long time. But when the stock market crashed in 1929 and the Great Depression ensued, charitable organizations were overwhelmed. Basically, they had functioned by soliciting donations from the wealthy, but now many of these well-to-do citizens were impoverished, too. The crash and subsequent bank failures wiped out the savings of countless families, wages plummeted, businesses closed at a frightening rate, and nationwide unemployment averaged 25 percent.

President Herbert Hoover refused to put more money into employment programs or relief—he was not about to turn the government into a welfare agency. But the Depression deepened, and by the end of his term, the embattled Hoover, a Republican, approved giving states big federal loans that were to be distributed to the needy. But it was too little, too late. Hoover was voted out of office—he was replaced by a Democrat, Franklin Delano Roosevelt.

In the mid-1930s, Roosevelt's New Deal programs set up Social

Security as old-age and disability insurance, not as a charity. Roosevelt also designated millions of federal dollars to programs that put people back to work, and he convinced states to start unemployment insurance. The U.S. government has been in the welfare business ever since.

Q Who was Montezuma, and why did he want revenge?

A As Fred Willard's character puts it in the movie *Waiting for Guffman*, "Montezuma's revenge is nothing more than good old-fashioned American diarrhea. Adult diapers should never enter the picture." More specifically, it's a general term for the diarrhea that afflicts about half of the tourists who visit Mexico and Central America, and it's caused by contaminated food and water. While the locals aren't totally immune, they have generally built up a better resistance to the disease-carrying microbes that are responsible for the runs.

The nickname, which became popular in the 1960s, refers to Montezuma II, a sixteenth-century Aztec emperor. From 1502 to 1520, Montezuma ruled the Aztec Empire in what is now southern Mexico, greatly expanding its reach and wealth by conquering other indigenous tribes. Everything was going swimmingly for Montezuma until the Spanish conquistador Hernán Cortés and his men showed up in 1519. According to some accounts, Montezuma and others believed that the Spaniards were gods whose coming was foretold by prophecy. But the Spaniards may have started this legend themselves after the fact. In any event, Montezuma welcomed Cortés and his men as honored guests and showered them with gifts.

Before long, Cortés had set his sights on claiming the Aztec land and the civilization's considerable gold for Spain. His first step was to capture Montezuma and hold him as a sort of hostage. By threatening Montezuma, Cortés attempted to subdue the Aztecs and persuade them not to resist the Spanish.

But many in the Aztec capital resented the Spanish and began to look down on Montezuma. When the Aztec people revolted against the conquistadors, Cortés commanded Montezuma to address the crowd and convince them to submit. Instead, they pelted Montezuma with stones. The emperor died three days later, though it's not clear whether his injuries were to blame or whether the Spanish executed him.

The revolt pushed the Spanish out of the capital, and eventually a new leader, Cuauhtemoc, took control to lead the resistance against Cortés. In the spring of 1521, the Spanish laid siege to the capital city; Cuauhtemoc and his people surrendered after several months. In just a few years, Cortés brought the Aztec Empire to an end.

So if the spirit of Montezuma is still lurking in Mexico, it makes sense that it might exact vengeance on foreign visitors. But if you're ever in Mexico, it's best not to joke about Montezuma's revenge. Jimmy Carter made that mistake on an official visit in 1979, sparking a minor international incident that hurt already strained relations with Mexican President José López Portillo. President Carter didn't mean anything by the comment, but the reaction was understandable. What nation wants to be known for inducing mass diarrhea?

Q Why are we supposed to remember the Alamo?

A The average three-year-old in Texas can probably tell you the tale of the Alamo, complete with names, dates, and cool sound effects. But it's understandable if the details are a little hazy for the rest of us. We have our own state histories to worry about.

The Alamo began as a Roman Catholic mission called Misión San Antonio de Valero, which was established by the Spanish in the early eighteenth century to convert Native Americans to Christianity. The missionaries moved out in 1793, and nine years later, a Spanish cavalry company moved in, turning it into a fort that it called the Alamo (after Alamo de Parras, the city in Mexico that had been the company's home base). When the Mexican War of Independence ended in 1821, Mexican soldiers had control of all of San Antonio, including the Alamo, and they built up the fort's defenses.

But no one cares if you remember any of this stuff. You're supposed to remember the Alamo because of what happened there during the Texas Revolution. This was a conflict between the Mexican government and the Texians—people who had moved to Mexican territory from the United States. The Texians chafed under the government of Mexican president General Antonio López de Santa Anna Pérez de Lebrón (or Santa Anna to his friends), who was trying to assert more central control over the region. The Texians rebelled against this crackdown and took control of San Antonio and the Alamo, among other places.

On February 23, 1836, General Santa Anna and thousands of soldiers showed up to reclaim the Alamo. William Travis, the commander of the Texian insurgents who held the Alamo, sent messengers out to request help from surrounding communities. He got only thirty-two more volunteers, bringing his fighting force up to about two hundred men. Though they were clearly outnumbered, Travis and his men decided that they would rather die than surrender the fort. They held out for thirteen days, but in a final assault on March 6, Santa Anna's soldiers took control of the fort and killed Travis and all of his men.

The defeat infuriated the Texian revolutionaries and strengthened their resolve. Two months later at the Battle of San Jacinto, Texian soldiers led by General Sam Houston shouted, "Remember the Alamo!" as they charged into the fray. The rebels defeated the Mexican army, captured Santa Anna, and won Texas its independence. "Remember the Alamo!" became a rallying cry, and the battle went down in history as a tale of brave men standing their ground against terrible odds.

The resulting Republic of Texas was short-lived and unstable, thanks in part to continued skirmishes with the Mexican army. On December 29, 1845, Texas became a U.S. state, and soon Mexico and the United States were embroiled in the Mexican-American War. But that's another story for another book. In the meantime, any Texas toddler should be able to tell you all about it.

Q Why did the Romans sell their urine?

A Because there was a demand for it. Why the demand? Because Romans used the stuff by the bucketful to clean and dye clothing. Why urine? Because it worked, it was plentiful, and it was cheap. Why did it work? Because the nitrogenous urea in urine generates ammonia when the urine is left standing around, and this ammonia is a disinfecting and bleaching agent.

Some Romans, like many other people of the time, used urine to wash their teeth, too. But before you go dissing the Romans, realize that for more than fifteen hundred years after the Roman Empire peaked, Europeans were still using urine to clean clothes. And the Romans were not slovenly people, relatively speaking. They were quite the scientists. For example, it's been argued that after the fall of Rome, battlefield medicine didn't return to Roman levels until World War I, and that's partly a function of hygiene. Besides, lots of people today drink their own urine in the name of alternative medicine.

The Romans made extensive use of public baths—a bit of a turn-off to many of us today, but actually a sign of their culture's advancement. (The Romans were great innovators in matters hydraulic, as evidenced by their clever work with aqueducts and plumbing.) In the first century AD, the emperor Vespasian enacted a "urine tax," and with it coined the proverb *pecunia non olet* ("money does not smell"). But pee does. Imagine the troughs at the more than one hundred public baths where urine vendors would collect their wares, which they sold to the multitude of establishments around Rome and elsewhere that cleaned and bleached and performed a kind of dry-cleaning on woolens. A significant number of Romans were employed in the cleaning industry, experts say.

All in all, we moderns would be astonished to learn how "green" the ancients were. They didn't pump crude oil from the earth and make gasoline of it, and they didn't make plastics of whatever it is we use to make plastics. No, they used what was at hand in remarkable ways. And considering how much urine is quite literally at hand, it's no surprise that they found a way to use it.

Q Why didn't the Vikings stay in North America?

A Because they weren't particularly good guests, and the Native Americans threw them out. According to ancient Norse sagas that were written in the thirteenth century, Leif Eriksson was the first Viking to set foot in North America. After wintering at the place we now call Newfoundland in the year 1000, Leif went home. In 1004, his brother Thorvald led the next expedition, comprised of thirty men, and met the natives for the first time. The Vikings attacked and killed eight of the nine native men they encountered. A greater force retaliated, and Thorvald was killed. His men then returned home.

Six years later, a larger expedition of Viking men, women, and livestock set up shop in North America. They lasted two years, according to the sagas. The Vikings traded with the locals initially, but they soon started fighting with them and were driven off. There may have been one further attempt at a Newfoundland settlement by Leif and Thorvald's sister, Freydis.

In 1960, Norse ruins of the appropriate age were found in L'Anse aux Meadows, Newfoundland, by Norwegian couple Helge and Anne Stine Ingstad. The Vikings had been there, all right. Excavations over the next seven years uncovered large houses and ironworks where nails and rivets were made, as well as woodworking areas. Also found were spindlewhorls, weights that were used when spinning thread; this implies that women were present, which suggests the settlement was more than a vacation camp.

The ruins don't reveal why the Vikings left, but they do confirm what the old sagas claimed: The Vikings were in North America. The sagas say that the settlers fought with the local *Skraelings,* a Norse word meaning "natives," until the *Skraelings* came at them in large enough numbers to force the Vikings out.

This sounds plausible, given the reputation of the Vikings—they'd been raiding and terrorizing Europe for centuries—and the Eriksson family's history of violence. Erik the Red, the father of Leif, founded a Greenland colony because he'd been thrown out of Iceland for murder, and Erik's father had been expelled from Norway for the same reason. Would you want neighbors like them?

Q Did someone else write Shakespeare's plays?

A For someone so famous, William Shakespeare remains a mysterious figure. Here's what we know:

He was born in Stratford-upon-Avon, England, in 1564 and died in 1616. He married when he was eighteen, his wife bore three children, and he lived apart from his family in London. Shakespeare left behind scant personal correspondence, but he gave the world thirty-eight plays, one hundred fifty-four sonnets, and two narrative poems. Thirty-six of the plays were published seven years after his death in what is now called the *First Folio.* He wrote romances, histories, comedies, tragedies, and "problem plays" (which can't really be characterized by any of the previous categories). The man was incredibly talented.

Or was he? Conspiracy theorists have alleged through the years that Shakespeare didn't write any of his plays and that they were really penned by, among others, Edward de Vere (also known as the Earl of Oxford), Sir Francis Bacon, Christopher Marlowe, or even Queen Elizabeth I. One prominent theory is that there are anagrams in the plays that, when decoded, reveal an author other than Shakespeare. Another is that Shakespeare was too uneducated to have written so wonderfully and that he was merely a front for a female or noble author. (It was considered uncouth in those days for such an esteemed person to write plays.)

So we ask: Did Shakespeare write his own material? The answer is yes...and no.

Upon arriving in London sometime around 1588, Shakespeare joined a theater company called Lord Chamberlain's Men, later renamed the King's Men. Shakespeare's plays were performed almost exclusively by this company. He was an actor, too, and appeared in his own and in other company members' plays. The creation of a play was (and still is) a collaborative effort. Copies of scripts were shared, commented upon, and edited. Once rehearsals began, scenes were deleted and changed. Even after a play premiered, it was subject to change.

Plays were the best entertainment available to the public in an era without video games, movies, television, and iPhones, but a company couldn't survive without constantly updating its offerings. As a result, there was enormous pressure for new material. And the plays were not actually owned by the playwright in the way we use a copyright today—the company owned the play. Shakespeare made his living by being a member of the company, not by writing any individual piece (although he was listed as the company's house playwright).

The point is, a number of people in the company would have provided input on Shakespeare's plays. That, however, is about as far as the conspiracy goes. Almost all academics today reject the notion that Shakespeare didn't write his plays, but as with shooters on the grassy knoll and UFOs in New Mexico, rumors persist in the popular mind. It's a plot device worthy of, well, Shakespeare.

Q Was there a real King Arthur?

A You've seen the movies: *Camelot, Excalibur, King Arthur*—even the Disney feature *The Sword in the Stone*. Is there truth behind the romantic myth of King Arthur? Of course. Can history prove that a good king named Arthur lived in England before, say, AD 1000? No.

Britain was part of the Roman Empire—perhaps an unwilling part—for nearly four centuries. In AD 410, though, Rome's control of the island shriveled and its armies withdrew. Chieftains and bands of lawless raiders fought for control. In the power vacuum that developed, an anti-Roman leader named Vortigern emerged to become king through acts of conspiracy and murder. A ruler with varying levels of reputation depending on the chronicler, Vortigern opened the door to Saxon mercenaries to help him repel Pict and Irish invaders. Ultimately, both the Saxons and the British turned on Vortigern, who burned to death in the castle in which he had taken refuge from his enemies.

A new leader rose to rally the many chieftains in England—a man named Ambrosius Aurelianus, who had led the British rebellion against Vortigern. Apparently born of a Roman or half-Roman family, Ambrosius imposed order in the countryside. He contained the Saxons and made the roads safe to travel. Peace settled on the land and trade flourished.

What does this have to do with Arthur? Ambrosius won the great Battle of Badon. Three accounts survive of this long-ago fight, and one of them credits a man named Arthur with victory. This account, written by the monk Nennius, who lived at least a hundred years later, says that at Badon, Arthur killed 960 men single-handedly, and that he won eleven other battles with the Saxons as well.

This seems to be the beginning of the legend. Many more years passed; Arthur the mighty warrior turned up in a few epics, legends, and poems from the British Isles. In the twelfth century, Geoffrey of Monmouth wrote the *History of the Kings of England,* in which Arthur is a mighty king with Guinevere at his side and Merlin serving as a prophet and advisor. How much of Geoffrey's work was based on histories and tales now lost? How much was his imagination? We do not know.

After Geoffrey, other writers, like Thomas Malory, embroidered what truth there was and turned it into marvelous, romantic fiction. Some of the stories of the Knights of the Round Table no doubt spring from older tales. The sword in the stone, for example, was an object worshipped a thousand years earlier by Sarmatian troops who were stationed in Britain by the Roman Empire.

The original Arthur probably did exist, but as a mighty war leader, not a king. The romance of Camelot, though, is wide open to interpretation. Since no one knows anything for sure, you can believe whatever you like.

Q Were the Viking beserkers really beserk?

A Depending on whom you ask, the Viking berserkers were either bloodthirsty thugs intent on pillaging everything in their path or an elite corps of buff warriors who had a hard time keeping their shirts on in the heat of battle.

The word "berserk" comes from Old Norse. It has been translated as "bare of shirt," meaning that the berserkers entered battle without armor and possibly bare-chested, or more literally as "bear-shirt," for the Vikings also liked to don the skins of their totem animals (bears and wolves). Sometimes they would even wear animals' heads as helmets or masks, the better to frighten their enemies. Such behavior jibes with the English definition of the word: "extremely aggressive or angry."

Vikings first sailed into European history in AD 793, when a group of longboats pulled up on the northeast coast of England right outside the abbey of Lindisfarne. Locals thought the boats—with their high, carved prows—were literally sea dragons and that the men who disembarked from them were equally possessed of supernatural powers.

After sacking Lindisfarne, the Vikings terrorized Europeans for the better part of the next two centuries, looting cities and villages, killing men, and seizing women and children and carting them off as slaves. The most fearsome of these raiders called themselves the sons of Odin. According to Norway's epic poet Snorri Sturluson, those who belonged to the cult of Odin "went to battle without armor and acted like mad dogs or wolves. They bit into their shields and were as strong as bears or bulls. They killed men, but neither fire nor iron harmed them. This madness is called berserker-fury."

How did they reach this state of madness or *berserkergang,* as the Scandinavians say? In 1956, psychiatrist Howard Fabing introduced the theory that the berserkers psyched themselves for battle with bites of *Amanita muscaria,* a potent hallucinogenic mushroom that is native to northern Europe. The notion that the Vikings owed their victories to psychedelic highs is intriguing, but it's unconvincing to many historians. Although the old Norsemen often went heavy on the mead (a fermented beverage made from honey), there's no archaeological evidence that they added mushrooms to their pre-battle menu.

Some scholars think that the berserkers may have been genetically prone to manic-depressive syndrome. Contemporary accounts depict them as swinging from states of wild rage to utter lassitude, a pattern in keeping with what we know of bipolar disorder. People in manic phases can experience huge releases of endorphins, which may explain why the berserkers seemed impervious to pain.

Or it is possible that the berserkers simply worked themselves into frenzied states through dancing, drumming, chanting, and other high-energy rituals. Whatever they did, it was certainly effective: The image of the Viking warrior has hardly dimmed through the ages, though their press has gotten slightly better. Today filmmakers are more apt to depict the berserker as a brave hero rather than a rapacious villain. And, of course, there are those fanatics in Minnesota who paint their faces purple just to watch football games. Now that's really berserk.

Q What are ziggurats?

A Everybody's heard of the pyramids of Egypt, but what about the ziggurats of Mesopotamia? Starting in the fourth millennium BC, more than two thousand years before the Egyptians built the Great Pyramid of Cheops, the Sumerians in Mesopotamia were busy constructing mighty towers in an attempt to reach all the way up to heaven. Or at least that's what the Bible tells us.

The word *ziggurat* comes from Akkadian, one of the earliest languages of the Near East. It means "to build on a raised area." Ziggurats resembled huge wedding cakes made of brick and clay. The tallest towers consisted of seven layers.

How high were these ziggurats? Not very, according to our standards. The temple of Borsippa, one of the largest ziggurats that has been excavated by archaeologists, is estimated to have stood 231 feet—or approximately 70 meters—high at completion. That's only a little less than a fifth as tall as the Empire State Building (1,250 feet) and less than one-fourth the height of the Eiffel Tower (984 feet). But on the relatively flat terrain of the Tigris-Euphrates valley, it's easy to see how that height would have impressed the locals.

Joseph Campbell, a famous scholar of world mythology, believed the ziggurats were regarded by the Sumerians as connectors between the earth and heaven. The lowest layers represented the original mound from which the earth was created, and the top layer served as a temple where the gods could dwell and look out over the land.

Did the Tower of Babel, a type of ziggurat, actually exist? About fifty to sixty miles south of contemporary Baghdad lie the remains of what archaeologists think is the ancient city of Babylon. There, they have uncovered the first layer of a temple whose name is *Etemenanki,* according to cuneiform tablets, which translates to "the foundation between heaven and earth." This temple must have been important because it was reconstructed several times over the centuries, most notably by King Nebuchadnezzar II around 600 BC.

Q What's so great about *Citizen Kane?*

A Every year since 1962, *Sight & Sound* magazine's poll of film critics has ranked *Citizen Kane* as the greatest movie of all time; many directors cite it as one of their chief influences and inspirations; and the American Film Institute put it at the top of its "100 Years, 100 Movies" list. Pretty impressive for a 1941 drama about a newspaper mogul that doesn't feature a single car chase, robot battle, or panty raid. What's the big deal, anyway?

Fans of *Citizen Kane* can give you dozens of reasons why they love it, citing everything from the screenplay to the sound design to the cinematography. And that's precisely why the movie is impressive: Orson Welles pulled out every innovative storytelling technique he could come up with to spin his yarn in an original, engaging way. It comes down to style—the movie is filled with creative filmmaking tricks.

Looking at the movie as a whole, what really sticks out is the unconventional way that the plot moves through time. The film begins with the death of the main character, Kane, and then cuts to an obituary newsreel that summarizes his rise and fall. The newsreel producer wants to know the meaning of Kane's final word, "rosebud," and sends a reporter out to investigate. As the reporter talks to everyone in Kane's life, the story unfolds through flashbacks, showing Kane at many ages and from many perspectives. In the first few minutes, you learn the basic story of Kane's life, but the true meaning comes out only as you double back and look closer through the multilayered memories of his friends and enemies. This was revolutionary in 1941. Fifty years before *Pulp Fiction*, Welles and the screenwriter Herman Mankiewicz jumbled up time and asked the audience to put it back together again.

When you examine the movie closely, you can see that just about every shot was meticulously crafted. Cinematographer Gregg Toland developed deep-focus techniques in order to create busy shots in which everything is in sharp focus, from objects right in front of the camera to people far in the background. Combined with extreme low- and high-angle shots, elaborate pans, symbolic imagery, creative sound editing, and rapid cuts through time, you end up with plenty to dissect.

The film received good reviews when it was released, but it was a bomb at the box office. In the 1950s, avant-garde European filmmakers rediscovered it and built on many of its ideas. By the 1960s, it was a standard subject in U.S. film schools, largely because it includes excellent examples of many filmmaking techniques. As a result, it left a mark on the generation of cutting-edge filmmakers that made the most important movies of the 1970s and 1980s.

But if you hate *Citizen Kane*, don't feel badly—several respected film critics do, too. Guess they like more panty raids in their art films.

Q Why does the Leaning Tower of Pisa lean?

A To understand why the tower leans, one should know the history of this remarkable crooked erection, including where it was built. At the turn of the first century AD, Pisa was a vibrant seaport city on the northwestern coast of Italy. In 1063, the Pisans attacked the city of Palermo. (And yes, this is where the phrase "Hey, Pisan!" comes from.) They were victorious and returned home with treasures.

The Pisans, being a proud people, wanted to show the world how important their city was, and decided to erect a great cathedral complex, called the Field of Miracles; the complex included a cathedral, cemetery, baptistery, and bell tower.

Pisa was originally named Poseidonia in 600 BC, from a Greek word meaning "marshy land." Bonanno Pisano, the original architect of the bell tower, did not think this was important information when he began the project. In 1173, Bonanno decided that since there was a good deal of water under the ground, he'd build a shallow foundation, one that was about three meters deep.

Five years later, when third-floor construction was about to begin, Bonanno realized that his structure was sinking on one side; this was because he built upon a bed of dense clay. But being a proud Pisan, he continued to go skyward. To attempt to solve the problem, he added two inches to the southern columns and thought no one would notice. People noticed. The third floor reached completion, and the job was halted indefinitely.

In 1272, construction of the bell tower resumed under the guidance of architect Giovanni di Simone. He completed four more floors, built at an angle to compensate for the listing. But not only did his remedy cause the tower to tilt in the other direction, but it also created a curve. In 1284, the job was once again halted. In 1319, the Pisans picked up their tools and completed the seventh floor. The bell tower was added in 1372, and then it was left to lean in peace until the nineteenth century.

In 1838, the foundation was dug out so visitors could see how it was built, which caused the tower to lean even more. Then in 1934, Benito Mussolini ordered the foundation to be reinforced with concrete. The concrete was too heavy, however, and it sunk the tower further into the clay.

Since then, many projects have come and gone; the tower is now stabilized and was reopened in 2001, so tourists can walk to the top. The Leaning Tower of Pisa is the top tourist attraction in Tuscany. The circular tower stands nearly 185 feet tall, is estimated to weigh almost sixteen thousand tons, has a 294-step spiral staircase, and leans at an angle of almost four degrees, meaning that the tower is about four meters off vertical. And to top it off, researchers from the University of Pisa found the tower to be sinking at a rate of one-twentieth of an inch annually. At that rate, they've predicted, the tower will collapse in fewer than three hundred years.

Q What's the difference between Cajun and Creole?

A Once, on a visit to a Louisiana bayou, an old Cajun said to us: "I got an ahnvee for some chee wee." We have no idea what that means, but such phrases are part of what makes Cajun culture—its language, its accordion-heavy music, and its crawfish étouffée—an integral part of the romance of New Orleans. The history of Louisiana Cajuns goes back to the French and Indian War of the mid-eighteenth century, when England and France battled over large swaths of colonial land, including what was then known as Acadia (now part of Nova Scotia, Canada).

Though Acadia was at that time part of a British colony, it was populated mostly by French settlers. Wary of having a colony full of French people during an impending war with France, the Brits kicked out everyone of French descent. These displaced settlers scattered all over North America, but a large percentage of them headed down to another French colony, Louisiana.

Though New Orleans was at that time a thriving port community, Acadians instead settled in the surrounding swampy, alligator-infested bayou regions. Through the years, the Acadians, or Cajuns, as they came to be known, developed a close-knit, if isolated, community with its own dialect, music, and folk wisdom. Technically, only people who are descended from the communities settled by those original displaced Acadians are considered Cajun.

Creole, on the other hand, can refer to any number of things. Originally the term, which dates back to the Spanish conquest of Latin America, meant any person descended from colonial settlers; eventually, any people of mixed race who were native to the colonies became known as Creoles. To add further confusion to the definition, there is something called a Creole language, which is most often born of the contact between a colonial language and a native one.

In Louisiana, Creole refers to people of any race born in Louisiana who descended from the original French settlers of the colony. These folks differ from Cajuns in that they came from places other than Acadia. Louisianan Creoles, too, have their own language—which differs from Cajun—that blends French, West African, and Native American languages; music (such as zydeco); and cuisine.

So there you have it—the difference between Cajun and Creole. Now you can think about something else the next time you're staggering down Bourbon Street.

Q Why do we call someone a dark-horse candidate?

A In 1831, Benjamin Disraeli (who became the British prime minister thirty-seven years later) used the term "dark horse" in a novel to describe an unknown horse that won a race and surprised everyone. After that, a dark horse could mean any contestant in sports or politics who didn't look promising but who might unexpectedly win.

In the 1844 U.S. presidential race, the expected nominee for the Democrats was Martin Van Buren. Van Buren argued against the annexation of Texas, though, which cost him the support of many delegates at the Democratic convention. There were no super delegates in those days, so the convention went through eight rounds of voting before the delegates selected a compromise candidate: James K. Polk, who had not even appeared on the first seven ballots. Months later, Polk was elected president. Since he literally came out of nowhere to win the ultimate prize, he is considered to be the first dark-horse candidate for president.

There have been others: James Garfield garnered the Republican nomination on the thirty-sixth ballot and won the general election by a scant ten thousand votes. When he was assassinated just months after taking office, his vice president, Chester Arthur, became president, which made him a sort of dark horse, too.

Not impressed? In 1860, an obscure Illinois lawyer came out of the woodwork to capture the nomination of the upstart Republican Party. Since the Democrats had split into factions, and the only other serious party, the Whigs, had collapsed, Abraham Lincoln became president. To many, he was the ultimate dark horse.

Q Did London Bridge really fall down?

A America is full of weird, wonderful tourist attractions. We've got the world's largest ball of twine built by one person (17,400 pounds) in Darwin, Minnesota; the world's largest office chair (thirty-one feet) in Anniston, Alabama; and the can't-miss RV Hall of Fame in Elkhart, Indiana. We've got enormous wheels of cheese, underground salt museums, and monumental Holstein cows. Perhaps the most surprising, though, is found in Lake Havasu, Arizona. That's where London Bridge—the same London Bridge of nursery rhyme fame—is located.

How London Bridge came to reside in one of the prime spring-break destinations for drunken college students is a long story, almost two thousand years long. In fact, the London Bridge on Lake Havasu is actually only one of many bridges that have borne the London name over the past two millennia. These bridges were made of timber, stone, and iron, but they all shared one trait: They fell down.

London Bridge's proud tradition of collapsing started with the first bridges over the River Thames (the river that cuts through London, for the geographically challenged), crude timber structures built starting in Roman times. After the Romans left, the first London Bridge, lonely and neglected, fell down. Over the next nine hundred years, a series of wooden bridges were erected and fell. But it wasn't until 1014 that the bridge collapsed dramatically enough for a nursery rhyme to be born.

In the late tenth and early eleventh centuries, England, ruled by the unfortunately named King Ethelred the Unready, was constantly besieged by Danish invaders. By 1014, Ethelred had had enough— he planned an attack that would drive the Danes out once and for all. Unfortunately, as Ethelred and his warriors rowed up the Thames, they were met by a hail of spears from Danish soldiers who had taken up a position on London Bridge.

Ethelred ordered his troops to tie ropes around the support beams and row away, thereby bringing the bridge down with them. It is this incident at which most folk etymologists point as the inspiration for the "London Bridge is falling down" nursery rhyme.

But what of the coda, "My fair lady?" It was probably added to the rhyme a few centuries after Ethelred took down the old London Bridge. By the late thirteenth century, London Bridge had been rebuilt twice (both of wood; both collapsed) before the English wised up and decided to use stone. At the time, Henry III was ruling England. He was not a particularly memorable ruler, but his wife was: Eleanor of Provence was one of the least popular queens in British history.

What made her even less popular was a gift she received from Henry III in 1269: all the toll money collected on London Bridge for the year. She quickly squandered it on personal possessions and her rather sizable retinue. Meanwhile, London Bridge, in dire need of repair, slowly crumbled. Hence, surly Londoners sang, "London Bridge is falling down, my fair lady." Yet somehow, despite a variety of natural and manmade disasters, this iteration of London Bridge lasted nearly six hundred more years.

In 1831, Eleanor's London Bridge was finally put out of its misery, and a new stone bridge, designed by John Rennie, was commissioned. In the 1960s, when the Brits decided to replace Rennie's stone structure with a modern bridge, they put the landmark up for sale.

In swooped American Robert McCulloch, who believed that the perfect place for London Bridge was Lake Havasu, Arizona, a city that he was essentially building from scratch as a tourist destination. The bridge was painstakingly disassembled and moved across the Atlantic, stone by stone, where it was reassembled and opened to the public as one of America's roadside attractions. It's no Giant Concrete Prairie Dog (Interior, South Dakota), but it's still worth a visit.

Q Did the Founding Fathers sleep around?

A Voting "nay" seems to make the most sense here. When it comes to the architects of the United States—particularly The Big Three: Thomas Jefferson, Benjamin Franklin, and George Washington—there is a lot more smoke than fire regarding their sexual antics. Beneath all the fancy tea drinking, powdered wigs, and frilly cravats, who would have thought these men could be considered the gossip targets of their day...and beyond?

When it came to scandal, Jefferson probably led the pack, with rumors of outside sexual dalliances following him during his life, and still today. Speculation of an extramarital affair with a slave whom he owned named Sally Hemings was supposedly put into motion as a selfish agenda by Richmond newspaper reporter James T. Callender. He published a claim that Jefferson was the father of five children by Hemings, including a son, Tom. Historians still hotly debate this topic. DNA testing in 2000 linked only one of Hemings' children to the Jefferson family. Was Thomas Jefferson the father? This isn't clear.

There's also a misconception about Franklin, the famed inventor and social philosopher. He allegedly made his rounds throughout France and America as quite the randy skirt-chaser. Depending on which rumor you believe, he fathered anywhere from thirteen to eighty illegitimate children. In actuality, he fathered only one illegitimate son, whose mother remains unnamed. The child was raised in a stable environment from infancy by Franklin and Franklin's common-law wife, Deborah Read. In short, there's no obnoxious Austin Powers resemblance here either.

As for the nation's first president, there have been rumblings that Washington fathered a child with a slave named Venus, who was owned by his half-brother John Augustine Washington. In 2004, Linda Allen Bryant, who is a descendent of West Ford, the named offspring, wrote a book declaring this association based on her family's oral history. Experts, however, have not found evidence to support the claim. As with Jefferson, someone in the Washington clan may have been the real father. For now, DNA testing has been shunned by the Mount Vernon Ladies Association, which cares for Washington's estate. Furthermore, West Ford's burial place is unknown, so tissue sampling isn't a possibility.

Washington planting his "seed" indeed would have been quite the eye-opener, considering historians believe he was probably sterile. Here's what we do know for sure: Washington enjoyed a happy married life with widowed Martha and helped to raise children from her previous marriage.

Oftentimes the truth isn't as sexy as rumors and innuendo.

Q What's the point of the electoral college?

A You've heard the mantra as each presidential election approaches: "Get out and vote! Every vote counts!" Well, guess what? That's not exactly true. Under the electoral college system, we don't elect the president through a direct, nationwide popular vote. The electoral college decides the outcome.

Just ask Al Gore. In the 2000 election, he beat George W. Bush in the nationwide popular ballot by more than five hundred thousand votes. However, in the electoral college, Gore was outdone by Bush, 271 to 266. And Bush was the new president.

This wasn't the only time a candidate who carried the popular vote didn't win a trip to the Oval Office. In 1888, Grover Cleveland got 90,596 more votes than Benjamin Harrison, but Harrison won the electoral college by sixty-five votes. In 1876, Samuel J. Tilden got 254,235 more votes than Rutherford B. Hayes, but Hayes prevailed in the electoral college—by one vote!

Are you wondering just who came up with this cockamamie system? The electoral voting process was designed by the framers of the U.S. Constitution (you know, our founding fathers). These political leaders believed that it was unfair to give Congress the sole power to select the president, but they also feared that a purely popular election would be reckless. (Ordinary citizens weren't considered to be informed enough to choose wisely.) And so they came up with the electoral voting system as a compromise.

Proponents of the electoral college system say that it works because a candidate must garner wide geographic support to win the presidency. They point out that it also protects the interests of smaller states that might otherwise be ignored if not for the power of their electoral votes. (Consider that if Gore had won tiny New Hampshire in 2000, the electoral vote would have swayed in his favor and he would have been president.)

Opponents of the electoral college argue that it's wholly undemocratic that the winner of the popular vote can lose the election. They also claim that there isn't an incentive for voters to turn out in states where one party is clearly dominant, and that the system penalizes third-party candidates. (In 1992, Ross Perot won a whopping 19 percent of the national popular vote, but he garnered no electoral votes.)

Is the electoral college fair? For the answer, we turn to the great Alexander Hamilton, an original proponent of the system, who said that the electoral college may not be perfect, but it's "at least excellent."

Q Why did Abraham Lincoln have an air corps?

A On June 18, 1861, Abraham Lincoln received an extraordinary message. "I have the pleasure of sending you this first telegram ever dispatched from an aerial station," his correspondent wrote, noting that from his vantage point, he could see the countryside surrounding Washington, D.C., for fifty miles in any direction. The "station" was an enormous hot-air balloon that was tethered across from the White House and hovering five hundred feet in the air. Thaddeus Lowe, the balloon's operator, had run a telegraph line from the passenger basket down to a ground cable that was connected to both the president and the Union Army War Office.

A self-taught scientist, engineer, and aeronaut, Lowe had been piloting balloons for a decade. He was also an ardent supporter of the Union. He had mounted his balloon demonstration because he wanted to serve his country—not on the ground, like other soldiers, but in the air. One of the Union's greatest fears was that the Confederacy would launch a sneak attack on Washington, D.C., via northern Virginia. Who better to keep an eye on enemy maneuvers, Lowe asked, than a spy in the sky?

Lincoln agreed. A few days later, on June 21, he created the Union Army Balloon Corps and appointed Lowe as its chief. Over the next two years, Lowe made three thousand balloon ascents. His telegraph apparatus relayed crucial information to the ground troops. During the Peninsula Campaign of 1861–62, Lowe alerted General George McClellan to the movements of rebel troops three miles away; it was the first time in history that a commander was able to use aerial intelligence to route an enemy. At the Battle of

Fair Oaks (May 31–June 1, 1862), Lowe's messages guided an entrapped Union battalion to safety.

Ever alert for new possibilities, Lowe also commandeered a barge from which he could make balloon ascents over the Potomac River, thus creating the first "aircraft carrier." His constant presence in the sky was such an irritant to the South that he became, according to author Carl Sandburg, "the most shot-at man of the Civil War." Though his balloon sailed too high for Confederate artillery to reach—the craft could climb to five thousand feet—Lowe did have a few close calls. At one point, he actually caught a cannonball in his basket.

Despite his daring, Lowe's balloon corps proved too controversial for the army. Rival balloonists, perhaps jealous of his success, accused him of mismanaging funds. Some generals found the balloons too cumbersome and expensive to transport. In addition, Lowe himself suffered ill health from a bout of malaria. The corps was officially disbanded in August 1863, and a disappointed Lowe returned to civilian life.

His exploits were not forgotten, however. He received the Franklin Institute's Grand Medal of Honor in 1886. A mountain near Pasadena, California, bears his name. And in 1988, he was posthumously inducted into the U.S. Military Intelligence Corps Hall of Fame, the sole balloonist among its honorees. It is a fitting tribute to the nation's original spy in the sky.

Q Why didn't George Washington sign the Declaration of Independence?

A At the bottom of the Declaration of Independence, you can see the names of a veritable all-star team of American patriots: John Hancock, whose gigantic signature suggests that he was something of a show-off; Benjamin Franklin, who was either mocking Hancock's signature or doing some less-graceful showing off of his own; Thomas Jefferson, the showoff who wrote the Declaration of Independence and made all the s's look like f's; and John Adams, who wasn't much of a showoff back then, but only because he didn't know that he would be the first of the signers to get his own HBO miniseries.

But the signature of the "Father of Our Country," George Washington, is conspicuously absent. That's right. Washington didn't chop down any cherry trees, didn't throw silver dollars across rivers, didn't wear wooden teeth, and didn't sign the Declaration of Independence.

Why is Washington's John Hancock missing from the document? Here's a refresher on American history: Washington served the colony of Virginia as a delegate to the Second Continental Congress when it convened in May 1775. A month later, the Congress appointed him Commander-in-Chief of the Continental Army. Washington's tenure as a member of the Continental Congress effectively ended when he was chosen to lead the army, which means that it wouldn't have been legally possible for him to sign the Declaration of Independence. He was replaced as a delegate to the Continental Congress approximately a month after his military appointment.

When the members of the Continental Congress began signing the Declaration of Independence in the summer of 1776, Washington was with his army in New York, preparing to defend the island of Manhattan against the British. If not for the deeds of Washington and his army throughout the American Revolution, the Declaration of Independence would have proved to be a worthless document. So in this instance, the sword was every bit as mighty as the pen.

Q Did P.T. Barnum really say, "There's a sucker born every minute"?

A Good old Phineas Taylor Barnum, the great-great-grandfather of the great all-American scam. The head huckster who told us, "There's a sucker born every minute."

Or did he?

Many contemporary historians believe that Barnum has been unfairly maligned. Rick Brown, founder of the Newspaper Collectors Society of America and Historybuff.com, fingers David Hannum as the real culprit. In 1869, Hannum was part of a group that was making a mint exhibiting a huge stone figure it claimed was a *bona fide* petrified giant, unearthed by a farmer in Cardiff, New York. Always on the lookout for new exhibits to add to his American Museum, Barnum offered fifty thousand dollars for the unusual specimen. (That's more than two million dollars today.)

When Hannum & Co. turned him down, Barnum "dug up" his own giant and announced that Hannum's was a fake. Hannum quickly retaliated with a lawsuit. Before the case could be resolved, amateur archaeologist George Hull came forward with the astounding confession that he himself had paid to have the Cardiff giant carved from gypsum, buried, and subsequently discovered. In other words, the whole thing was a hoax. Somewhere in this comedy of errors, Hannum is reputed to have said, "There's a sucker born every minute."

It's also possible that the famous saying came from Joseph Bessimer, otherwise known as "Paper Collar Joe," a notorious con man of the late nineteenth century. Joe may have had a paper collar, but unfortunately, he left no paper trail to document his statement, so we're stuck with historical rumor.

Why is the quote attributed to Barnum? Adam Forepaugh, a rival circus owner, may have attributed the words to Barnum in the 1880s in an attempt to smear his competitor's reputation.

Legendarily, Barnum wasn't above pulling a few fast ones. He posted a sign at his sideshow that read, "This Way to the Egress," banking on the assumption that most visitors wouldn't know "egress" is a synonym for "exit" and wouldn't find out until they were back out on the street and had to pay for another ticket if they wanted to continue their tour.

But Barnum knew where to draw the line. He was a believer in what he called "humbug," or the art of putting on "glittering appearances." Humbug was not out-and-out dishonesty—it was entertainment. "I don't believe in duping the public, but I do believe in first attracting them and then pleasing them," he wrote to a publisher in 1860. People wouldn't mind being deceived, he surmised, as long they felt they had gotten their money's worth.

How right was he? It's easy to test his hypothesis. Your laboratory is right in your living room. It's called TV.

Q Is there more to Oktoberfest than drinking beer?

A Of course, *meine Freundin*. Bavarian beer is certainly a main attraction at Oktoberfest, but there are plenty of other things to do. For starters, you could learn a little German. Lesson one: While most of the world knows this famous festival as Oktoberfest, Munich, Germany, locals actually call it *die Wiesn*. Literally translated, that means "the meadow" or "the field," and refers to the fields in front of the Munich city gates where the original Oktoberfest was held. More on that later.

Another word you should know is *riesnbrezn*. These are the beloved, behemoth pretzels sold on the *Wiesn* fairgrounds. Come on, what goes better with beer than pretzels? How about roasted duck, dumplings, cheese, noodles, potato salad, oxtails, sauerkraut, sausage, pork knuckles, and grilled fish-on-a-stick? These German foods are just as much a part of the Oktoberfest tradition as the one-litre tankards of Augustiner, Hacker-Pschorr, Hofbräu, Löwenbräu, Paulaner, and Spaten—the only beers that are allowed to be served at the Munich Oktoberfest.

As for events, the main attraction is the Oktoberfest Costume and Riflemen's Parade, which is on the first *Wiesn* Sunday. It's a seven-kilometer stretch of men dressed in lederhosen, ladies dressed in dirndls, and about seven thousand performers who look like they've stepped out of Hansel and Gretel's gingerbread house.

Of course, none of this frivolity could get going without an official opening ceremony. On the first day of Oktoberfest, at precisely noon, the mayor of Munich traditionally taps the first keg and calls out, "*O'zapft is!*" This confirms a successful tap; it's only after the mayor's decree that the tents may begin serving beer. And serve they will, beginning as early as 9:00 A.M. on the weekends and 10:00 A.M. during the week.

It's true: Beer is an important aspect of the Oktoberfest tradition. In fact, over the course of this sixteen-day party, about 30 percent of the year's production of Munich breweries will be consumed. But truly, all this merriment is tied into an almost two-hundred-year-old celebration of cultural heritage.

It all began with a wedding. The first Oktoberfest was held on October 12, 1810, to honor the marriage of Bavarian Crown Prince Ludwig to Princess Therese von Sachsen-Hildburghausen. Prince Ludwig invited all the citizens of Munich to attend the royal event, which was held on the fields in front of the city gates. He organized days of festivities, including a horse race and superabundant amounts of beer and food.

In the following years, Prince Ludwig's celebration was repeated every October. Nowadays, Oktoberfest is somewhat more of a Septemberfest—the event begins in late September and carries into October. September nights in Munich are a little warmer, so visitors can stroll *die Wiesn*, eat their *riesnbrezn*, and of course, drink their Löwenbräu for longer into the night. *Prost!*

Chapter 4
INCREDIBLE EDIBLES

Q What is the record for the most milk from a cow?

A Number 289 may not have looked like much, but she was a real cash cow. Owned by M. G. Maciel & Son Dairy of Hanford, California (which did not name its animals), number 289 produced 465,224 pounds of milk during her lifetime (1964–1984). How many gallons is that? Get out your calculator.

One gallon of milk weighs about 8.6 pounds. So number 289, a Holstein breed, produced about 54,070 gallons in her lifetime. Given that cows start lactating around age two, that works out to 3,004 gallons a year. To make things a little more complicated, dairy farmers often prefer to measure milk production in lactation cycles, which are ten months long. Using this standard, 289 cranked out 2,503 gallons per cycle.

As you can see, measuring milk is not a simple process. While number 289 may hold the lifetime record, the record for the most milk produced in one year was set by a Holstein named Lucy, of the LaFoster Dairy in North Carolina. In 1998, she produced 75,275 pounds of milk, or roughly twenty-four gallons per day. The previous annual record was held by another Holstein, Ellen, of Fulton County, Indiana; she produced 55,560 gallons in 1973. Ellen's all-time daily high was twenty-three gallons, in January 1975.

The Dairy Herd Improvement Association (DHIA), however, does not recognize number 289 as the all-time champion, because the agency did not record her milk production. The DHIA's champ is Granny, of Koepke Farms Incorporated in Oconomowoc, Wisconsin. Granny produced 458,609 pounds of milk, or about 53,327 gallons, before she died in June 2006 at the age of twenty.

How do these heavyweights compare to the average heifer? According to the DHIA, a healthy dairy cow can produce between 17.4 and 20.9 gallons per day when lactating. For most cows, that's about 305 days per year. Statistics from the U.S. Department of Agriculture reveal that in 2007, an active dairy cow averaged 20,267 pounds of milk. When you consider that dairy cows in 1900 produced fewer than ten thousand pounds annually, you can see that we are living in a land flowing with milk, if not honey.

The 1994 introduction of bovine somatotropin, commonly known as bovine growth hormone (BGH), has no doubt been responsible for some of the surge in milk production. Although there isn't proof that BGH is a health risk for cows or people, its use has sparked considerable controversy. Are champion milk cows that are given BGH the bovine equivalent of human athletes on steroids? That's an issue that can be argued until, well, the cows come home.

Meanwhile, whether you prefer organic or hormonally enhanced milk, you can lift a glass of the white stuff in honor of number 289, who did her thing the old-fashioned way. Like any true champ, her number has been retired back in Hanford.

Q Who invented food-on-a-stick?

A Corn dogs, popsicles, cotton candy, and candy apples—some of America's best treats are served up on a stick. Really, what's more fun than kabobbing around a summer carnival with a stick of corn in one hand and cheesecake-on-a-stick in the other?

How about adding fried pickles, sloppy joes, alligator sausage, or spaghetti and meatballs to your food-on-a-stick shtick? At the Minnesota State Fair, held annually over Labor Day weekend, you'll find some sixty-nine different foodstuffs that are offered up on a stick, ranging from the traditional to the completely outlandish. Corned beef and cabbage on a stick? You got it. Don't forget to wash it all down with an espresso-on-a-stick—frozen espresso, of course.

Yep, those Minnesota State Fair vendors have taken the food-on-a-stick concept to a whole new level of culinary genius. But the truth is, people have been using sticks, skewers, poles, and spits to cook and serve up food for centuries. That's why it's so confoundingly difficult to say who came up with the idea in the first place.

Most people agree that the original food-on-a-stick was probably the shish kebab. But who invented the kebab? Some say that it was the nomadic Turkish soldiers who invaded and conquered Anatolia—the heartland of modern-day Turkey—in the eleventh century. According to legend, these warriors used swords to grill their meat over their campfires as they moved westward from Central Asia.

But don't tell that to the Greeks—or to Mediterranean food expert Clifford A. Wright. According to this James Beard Foundation Award winner, there's plenty of iconographical evidence to suggest that the ancient Greeks were skewering up shish kebabs as early as the eighth century BC, well before the Turks blazed their destructive (yet tasty) trail into the region. Want proof? Just dig up your copy of Homer's *The Odyssey*.

We may never know the true inventor of the concept, but one thing's for sure: Food-on-a-stick is popular in almost every culture in the world. The Japanese have their yakitori, the French have their brochettes, and we have our Pronto Pups.

But who exactly invented that quintessentially American cornbread-coated wiener-on-a-stick? As you might expect, this question is hotly debated. Claimants to the title include Jack Karnis, the Fletcher brothers (Carl and Neil), and the Cozy Dog Drive In of Springfield, Illinois.

Who knew food-on-a-stick could be such a sticky subject?

Q How do restaurants make money on all-you-can-eat buffets?

A Go holler, "Feast!" and watch the egg rolls fly. Behold the buffet, humankind's magnificent shrine to bountiful banquets and conspicuous crapulence, all for a nominal fee. But while watching the masses devour heaping helpings of food from king-size self-serve stations is a compelling spectacle, it's equally remarkable to discover that some restaurants profit from this bargain-priced gluttony.

How so? It starts with labor costs. Servers at all-you-can-eat restaurants don't have to take orders and deliver food; all that is needed are people to clear plates from the table, fill drinks (this task isn't even necessary at restaurants that have self-serve drink stations), and replenish the buffet. This means that fewer employees can tend to more tables, and those tables turn over more quickly than at a normal restaurant because there is no wait for food—an equation that contributes to the financial success of all-you-can-eat establishments.

Menu options are another factor. Quantity, not quality, is king in the buffet line—in other words, you're not going to find haute cuisine at Old Country Buffet. Some dollars may be lost when diners go nuts on the more costly dishes, like meat and seafood, but that deficit is counterbalanced by the people who fill up on the bounty of less expensive fare, such as potatoes and other starches. Besides, restaurants have some tricks to guard against overindulgence, such as providing smaller plates and utensils, and pre-plating meat and seafood items.

Pricing proves to be the trickiest part of the equation. A restaurateur must measure the cost of serving each dish against the amount that is consumed. These numbers yield a usage history and enable the restaurant owner to calculate future costs and revenue. As is the case with just about everything these days, restaurateurs can use computer software to determine their various food formulas.

Thanks to a program called EatecNetX, a feast of information—such as how many servings of an item were prepared on a given day, how many were consumed, and even what time the dish ran out—is merely a few keystrokes away. So is important minutia, like how much of various ingredients needs to be on hand in the kitchen to prepare a certain number of servings of a dish.

It isn't all chicken wings and smiles in the buffet biz. In their quest to uphold the bottom line, some restaurant owners have ruled their buffets with an iron fist, denying certain customers service, asking others to leave after reaching a designated food limit, or tacking extra charges onto bills. These don't seem like wise practices, considering the all-you-can-eat business is predicated on allowing customers to stuff their faces with impunity. No one goes to a buffet to eat, drink, and be wary.

Q Saccharin, Splenda, Equal— what's the difference?

A Let's throw in cyclamates, too. Are all of these artificial sweeteners the same? No. They differ in taste and strength, and possibly in their effect on the human body. But most of us can't keep them straight.

Saccharin was the first artificial sweetener that was discovered, back in 1879. Chemist Constantin Fahlberg, while working on coal-tar derivatives, went home from his lab at Johns Hopkins University with something on his hands that tasted sweet. After Fahlberg patented saccharin, his mentor asserted that he was the one who had spilled saccharin on Fahlberg's hands, but it didn't do him any good. Fahlberg kept the patent and the profits.

And there were profits. Although saccharin was banned briefly, starting in 1912, from foods in the United States because of questions about its wholesomeness, World War I caused sugar shortages and the ban was lifted. Saccharin sales took off. After decades of popularity, saccharin was banned again when it was removed from the government's list of safe substances in the 1970s. In 1977 the ban was replaced with a warning label about its potential dangers, and in 1996 Congress repealed the requisite warning notice on items that contain saccharin. However, saccharin has been banned in Canada since 1977.

Other sweeteners were discovered in much the same way: Scientists spilled things in their labs and realized the spills tasted sweet. In 1937, a graduate student at the University of Illinois discovered cyclamate when he picked up his cigarette from a lab bench. He'd been working on anti-fever drugs. In 1965, aspartame got on the fingertips of a chemist who was researching ulcer treatments for the G. D. Searle Company. In 1976, a London graduate student at King's College confused a request for "testing" as "tasting" and discovered sucralose while doing some work for Tate & Lyle, a sugar company.

We see the results of these discoveries every time we go into a coffee shop. The pink Sweet 'N Low packet is saccharin, the blue Equal is aspartame, and the yellow Splenda is sucralose.

The products are not equally sweet. Saccharin is three hundred times sweeter than sugar, and aspartame/Equal is one hundred sixty to two hundred times sweeter and lacks a bitter aftertaste. Sucralose/Splenda is six hundred times sweeter than sugar, so it is mixed with fiber to give it some volume.

And cyclamate? It's only thirty to forty times sweeter than sugar. Cyclamate, one of the original ingredients in Sweet 'N Low, was banned by the U.S. Food and Drug Administration after controversial tests linked the substance to cancer in lab rats. It is marketed in other countries as Sugar Twin. (In the United States, Sugar Twin is saccharin.)

Although tests on those pitiful lab rats frequently raise cancer scares, sugar-free products are big business. Nearly two hundred million Americans eat or drink sugar-free foods. Diet soda, for example, accounted for nearly 30 percent of all soft drink sales in 2007—and Americans spent about seventy billion dollars on soft drinks. Soda companies obviously don't need sugar in order for their sales to be sweet.

Q Why is bottled water so expensive?

 You're on road trip. You've stopped to fill up your car with gas, and you duck inside to buy a few snacks and a drink.

You trot back to your car with Ding Dongs, Doritos, and a bottle of water in hand. You get inside the car, and then it hits you so hard that the airbags deploy: That bottle of water you just bought cost more per gallon than the gas!

Outrageous? Sure. Premium bottled water can cost up to ten dollars per gallon. But believe it or not, there is a method to the madness. You would think that there would be little work—and in turn, little expense—involved in processing water, but this isn't the case. In fact, the process is nearly identical to that of making Coca-Cola;

both beverages are treated at a plant, bottled, packaged, and shipped to stores.

Still, is premium bottled water (such as Aquafina and FIJI, which cost six to seven dollars a gallon) really better than the entry-level offerings (such as Acadia Spring, which goes for less than one dollar a gallon)? Absolutely not. Test after test has indicated that there's no difference in quality or taste among bottled waters.

In fact, it's possible that some premium and entry-level waters are culled from the same sources. The difference in water prices can be explained in the same way as any generic-versus-name-brand comparison: marketing. The prices have little to do with quality or taste, and everything to do with status and perception.

What sets water apart from every other beverage on the market is that consumers can access it from their own home taps, essentially for free ($.002 a gallon). Numerous studies have demonstrated that water from home taps is just as clean as bottled water. In fact, because the Environmental Protection Agency and local municipalities regulate the water supply more stringently than the Food and Drug Administration (FDA) monitors food and beverage producers, tap water is often much more pure and free of bacteria than bottled water. Amazingly, the FDA requires no testing whatsoever for sparkling water.

Don't be deceived into thinking that the pastoral picture on the bottle's label is an accurate snapshot of where it originated. More than 25 percent of so-called spring waters are culled from the same sources as your tap water. Aquafina and Dasani, the two top-selling bottled waters, are simply tap water with a screw-top; Aquafina comes from—of all places—the Detroit River.

There's also a different kind of expense attached to bottled water—the environmental cost of creating millions of plastic bottles, about 80 to 90 percent of which end up in landfills rather than recycling plants. That's four billion bottles in the waste stream every year, which costs cities seventy million dollars annually to clean up and bury in landfills. As a result, Chicago and many other cities have begun levying a bottle tax on plastic water bottles to offset these costs.

But the price tag rings high well before the bottle lands in the trash bin. Manufacturing and shipping those petroleum-based containers costs the real-dollar equivalent of seventeen million barrels of oil per year, which is enough fuel to power one million cars for a year.

The environmental cost of a single $1.50 bottle of FIJI water—that's culling the water; creating, filling, and packaging the bottle; and shipping it to a consumer in the United States—is 7.1 gallons of water, .26 gallon of fossil fuel, and 1.2 pounds of greenhouse gas emissions.

The moral of this story? The hefty price tag on a bottle of water at your local convenience store is only a fraction of its true cost.

Q Do poppy seed muffins cause positive drug tests?

A Yes. Next time you enjoy a slice of poppy seed cake with ice cream, you can say, "This will go straight to my hips...and straight from my urine to a positive drug test in a lab." We can't guarantee that you won't lose invitations to social events after the comment, but you won't be lying.

Depending on when you take the test, simply eating one poppy seed bagel can lead to a positive result. Such a finding is often referred to as a "false positive." This term, however, is false in itself: The test comes back "positive" because you do have morphine in your system. But the reason you test positive is what your employer or parole officer cares about: Were you chasing the dragon or chasing the complete breakfast?

Poppy seeds contain morphine, but after being gobbled up, they don't have any drug-related effect on the body. However, the morphine is detectable in your urine, and there's no way to tell from a basic urine test whether the morphine came from heroin or a muffin.

To address this curious problem, the legal threshold for a positive drug-test result was raised in 1998. The Mandatory Guidelines for Federal Workplace Drug Testing Programs adjusted the point at which a test is considered "positive" from three hundred nanograms per milliliter to two thousand nanograms per milliliter. This revised threshold does miss a few drug abusers, but it filters out most of the positive results that are caused by the munchies. Additionally, hair testing can help to clarify which type of morphine is detected.

The type of poppy seed that is consumed and where it was grown can also affect drug-test results. Spanish poppy seeds, for example, contain more morphine than Turkish poppy seeds. Your body isn't able to tell the difference, but your urine apparently can.

Q If an animal is stressed before being slaughtered, will it taste worse?

A Let's say you're driving down the highway and you see one of those trucks full of cattle. There are certain people (you know who you are) with a personality trait—let's call it a "sense of humor," for lack of a better term—that compels them to try to arouse a response from those cows, maybe by doing something like yelling, "Mooooo!"

Well, stop it. You think you're being funny, but you're really just ruining someone's dinner.

Those cows are going to the slaughterhouse. Remember how you felt back in school (we're guessing college) when the teacher told you to stop making farting noises with your armpit? You felt picked on, stressed out—maybe even a little angry. That's something similar to how a cow feels when it's been rounded up with a bunch of other confused cows and taken away from its familiar surroundings in a giant, noisy machine. Livestock such as cows, pigs, and sheep can get stressed, and when stressed-out livestock becomes meat, it tastes bad.

When an animal is stressed—psychologically (say, by mooing motorists or by other disruptions experienced on the way to the slaughterhouse) or physically (say, by fighting, which happens when animals are put in pens with other animals they don't know)—it gets tense, worn out, or exhausted. This causes the glycogen stores, or short-term energy, in its muscles to be used up.

If the animal is slaughtered before the glycogen levels are restored, the meat will have a high pH level, or not enough lactic acid.

In the meat-processing industry, this is known as dark, firm, dry (DFD) meat. DFD meat is sticky and has less flavor. It is also more susceptible to microorganisms, which makes its shelf life dangerously short. Another related condition is pale, soft, exudative (PSE) meat. PSE meat, most commonly pork, drips and is soft and mushy. *Mmmmmm!*

Good livestock handlers go to great lengths to ensure that their animals remain as stress-free as possible before slaughter. These measures include hearty meals and plenty of rest for the condemned beasts. After all, nothing is worse for the meat business than bad taste.

Q What does humble pie taste like?

A Which would you rather swallow: your pride or a mouthful of deer gizzard? Actually, original recipes for humble pie included the heart, liver, and other internal organs of a deer, or even a cow or boar. Talk about your awful offal!

The term "humble pie" derives from "umble pie," which dates back roughly to fourteenth-century England. The term "numbles," then later "umbles," referred to those aforementioned, um, select bits of a deer carcass. Umble pie was eaten by servants, whose lords feasted on the more palatable cuts of venison or whatever beast was being served. If meat was on the menu and you were eating umble pie, you were likely to be in a lower or more inferior position in society. The transition from the original term to the pun "humble pie" was an easy one, given that some English dialects silence the "h" at the beginning of a word.

For some unfathomable reason, modern-day recipes for humble pie do exist, although these call, mercifully, for cuts of beef or other meat. Others are more customary dessert pies with sweet fillings that inspire humility only when you're in the presence of a bathroom scale.

So the next time you've done somebody wrong, just apologize, take your lumps, wait for time to heal the wound, and consider yourself fortunate. It's better to spend "thirty days in the hole," to quote the 1970s British supergroup Humble Pie, than to eat a boar's intestines.

Q What is the tastiest part of the human body for cannibals?

A This question gets asked all the time. After all, what if the plane carrying your national rugby team crashes in the mountains, as happened to the Uruguayan team in 1972? Or your wagon train is trapped for the winter on a desolate mountain pass, like the infamous Donner Party? You may need to know just which cuts of human flesh are the tastiest in such situations.

Unfortunately, *Bon Appétit* has yet to publish its "Cannibal" issue—the headline will be easy to write: EAT ME! So we're forced to go to primary sources to determine which parts of the human body are the most succulent. Fortunately, there aren't many of them.

According to archaeological evidence, human cannibalism has a long history that dates back to the Neanderthals. Despite the stereotype that cannibals only live on remote islands, or in the deepest jungles, evidence of cannibalism has been found in cultures on nearly every continent, including Europe and North America. However, most cannibalistic practices throughout history were of a ritual nature, and there were few food critics writing up snappy reviews of their human feasts. For that, we have to consult those individuals throughout history who dined on other humans for pleasure.

The current living expert on cannibalism—Armin Meiwes, the German cannibal who is serving a life sentence for devouring a willing victim—likened the taste of his "cannibalee" to pork. Meiwes prepared his meal in a green pepper sauce, with a side of croquettes and Brussels sprouts. Science seems to agree with Meiwes. Some Japanese researchers manufactured "an electromechanical sommelier," a kind of gastronomist robot capable of sampling wines, cheeses, meats, and hors d'oeuvres, and identifying what it has been fed. When one reporter stuck his hand in the robot's maw, the two-foot robot immediately identified it as prosciutto. When the accompanying cameraman offered his hand, the mechanical gourmand declared, "Bacon."

So, what is the tastiest part of the human body? That seems to be a matter of debate. Early twentieth-century murderer and cannibal Albert Fish declared that the buttocks were the choicest cut, but latter-day cannibal Sagawa Issei disagrees, claiming that the thighs get that honor. In Fiji, where cannibalism was practiced until the late 1860s, men (women apparently were forbidden from partaking in this tasty treat) also favored the thighs (they also preferred the flesh of nonwhite women).

So if you really must know, there you have it: The thighs and buttocks are the prime cuts of a human. Just don't invite us to dinner.

Q What's the world's most fattening food?

A You know what? Technically speaking, any food can be fattening if you eat too much of it and exceed your daily caloric needs. Bananas may be healthy, but eat twenty of them, and we're talking 2,100 calories! The average person only needs about 1,400 to 2,000 calories per day.

Okay, if you're like most people, you're not going to go that bananas for bananas. But a double bacon cheeseburger sure sounds good, doesn't it? So let's focus on those high-fat, high-calorie dishes we all love to indulge in, especially when eating out. Ready to order your triple-bypass special?

According to a lineup of "The Best (Worst) Foods" compiled by Forbes.com in 2005, the most fattening food in the world is—drum roll, please—eggs Benedict. Typically an English muffin topped with ham or Canadian bacon, poached eggs, and hollandaise sauce, the average single serving of eggs Benedict contains one thousand calories and seventy-two grams of fat.

Most of the artery-clogging, cellulite-inducing fat and cholesterol in this dish come from the hollandaise—a rich emulsion of egg yolks and butter with a hint of fresh lemon juice and cayenne pepper. Just so you know, dietary guidelines established by the United States Department of Agriculture (USDA) say the recommended daily value of saturated fat for the average two-thousand-calorie diet is less than twenty grams per day. So eat seventy-two grams of fat with your eggs Benedict for breakfast, and you've overblown your daily blubber budget by 9:00 A.M.

Others on the Forbes.com list include duck confit (60 grams of fat, 1,000 calories), cheese fondue (50, 1,300), foie gras (35, 350), fettuccine Alfredo (40, 500), lasagna (30, 500), and General Tso's chicken (28, 400).

On the American restaurant front, there are plenty of places to point your bloated finger. Our favorite fast-food joints seem to be heavily engrossed in a battle over just who can come up with the most fattening food. At Hardee's, for instance, you'll find the Monster Thickburger. The restaurant chain describes it as "Two ⅓-lb. 100% Angus Beef Patties, Bacon, American Cheese and Mayonnaise on a Buttered, Seeded Bun." According to Hardee's nutritional data, this beast comes in at 1,420 calories and 108 grams of fat. What could be worse for you?

Check out "The 20 Worst Foods in America," as compiled by *Men's Health* magazine in 2008. Its pick for fat champ? Outback Steakhouse's Aussie Cheese Fries with ranch dressing. With 2,900 calories and 182 grams of fat, this appetizer is the equivalent of eating fourteen Krispy Kreme doughnuts in one sitting. Even if you share with a mate or two, you're looking at a surefire spare tire. *Bon appétit!*

Q Who's Mary, and how'd she get so bloody?

A If you're a student of history, you'll know that "Bloody Mary" is the nickname that was given to Mary Tudor. As the first queen to rule England (1553–1558), Mary Tudor is best remembered for the brutality of her effort to re-establish Catholicism as the religion of the state. (She was trying to undo the change that her father, Henry VIII, had made when he dissed the pope, divorced Mary's mother, and got hitched—if we can believe Hollywood—to Natalie Portman.) Mary Tudor's plan involved hanging non-Catholics, rebels, and heretics from the gibbet and burning nearly three hundred others at the stake. It's little wonder that she was given such an unpleasant moniker.

But for those of us who are less historically minded, the words "Bloody Mary" conjure a much more pleasant image: no roasting of Protestants, just a delicious glass of spicy tomato juice and vodka. So how did such a terrifying monarch inspire such a tasty drink?

It seems that the name of this popular barroom beverage has been connected to a number of historical and fictional women. By most popular accounts, the Bloody Mary was indeed named for Mary I, England's royal slaughteress. However, others associate the Bloody Mary with everyone from Hollywood actress Mary Pickford to the beheaded Mary, Queen of Scots, to Mary Worth (according to an urban legend, a child-murdering witch who will scratch your eyes out when summoned to your bathroom mirror).

The truth is, the Bloody Mary's creator, Fernand Petiot, had none of these women in mind when he concocted the original tomato juice and vodka cocktail at Harry's New York Bar in Paris in the 1920s. Petiot said, "One of the boys suggested we call the drink 'Bloody Mary' because it reminded him of the Bucket of Blood Club in Chicago, and a girl there named Mary."

Interestingly, when Petiot moved from his post in Paris to the King Cole Bar at the St. Regis in New York in 1934, the hotel tried to change the name of his Bloody Mary to Red Snapper (the term "bloody" was considered a tad rude in certain sophisticated circles), but the new name never stuck. Over time, Petiot modified the drink, spicing it up with black and cayenne pepper, Worcestershire sauce, lemon, and Tabasco sauce.

Today, more than a million Bloody Marys are served every day in the United States. Whether garnished with a celery stick, pickle, lemon, or lime, one thing's for sure: This blood-red cocktail is bloody good. Cheers to you, Mary.

Q Why do round pizzas come in square boxes?

A Here's a question that comes up virtually every time we order a pizza—which, considering our waistlines, is far too often.

According to pizza-packaging historians (yes, they do exist), the first pizza boxes were probably developed after World War II, when the popularity of takeout pizza rose dramatically. The first boxes weren't really boxes at all, but pizza placed on chipboard or corrugated cardboard and slid into a paper bag, which was subsequently taped or stapled shut. (Some longtime pizzerias still use this method.) There were a number of obvious drawbacks to this method. First, a paper bag doesn't retain heat very well, so unless you brought the pizza straight home, you'd find a congealed mess. Second, the paper bag tended to stick to the top of the pizza, so you needed to pry half of the toppings off the paper before eating the congealed mess. Third, there was no way to stack the pizzas if you were trying to carry more than one.

Pizza vendors looked for an answer—and they looked hard. Enter the square cardboard box. Though the first pizza boxes looked more like bakery boxes—you know, those flimsy white boxes that usually hold sheet cakes decorated with massive blue flowers—the

corrugated cardboard box of modern times soon became the package of choice. When Domino's Pizza began in 1960, the proprietors chose these square boxes as the basis for their pizza delivery system. Square boxes provided many advantages: They were easy to stack, they were durable, and they kept the pizza warm longer.

Nowadays, square boxes persist for a number of reasons. From a marketing perspective, a square box provides the illusion of a larger, better-value pizza. (Indeed, when Domino's experimented with an octagonal box in the 1990s, rival Pizza Hut immediately launched an ad campaign claiming that Domino's was "cutting corners.") In addition, a square box provides more square footage for advertising and logo display.

Finally, we are a nation that enjoys dipping sauces. Where in a circular box do you expect pizza makers to put our dipping sauces? We need our dipping sauces! Speaking of which...where is that pizza guy?

Q Why does bottled water have a "best if used by" date?

A In the United States, bottled water is considered a packaged food. Thus, it is regulated by the U.S. Food and Drug Administration (FDA). According to the FDA's Current Good Manufacturing Practices (CGMP), all bottled water must be sampled, analyzed, and found to be safe and sanitary. CGMP regulations also specify proper bottling procedures, record keeping, and plant and equipment design.

And that's not all. Bottled water must adhere to state regulations, and bottled-water producers that are members of the International Bottled Water Association must follow that trade organization's code, which runs a stupefying thirty pages. The different ways that bottled water can be described on the label include: spring water, purified water, mineral water, distilled water, drinking water, and artesian water. According to the FDA, carbonated water, seltzer water, soda water, sparkling water, and tonic water are soft drinks, so they are not regulated as bottled water.

What does all of this have to do with the "best if used by" date on many of the bottles of water that are consumed in the United States? Plenty. Bottled water that meets FDA requirements has an indefinite shelf life, according to the agency. Therefore, the FDA does not require bottlers to list a "best if used by" date on approved water, nor does it require an expiration date.

With bottled water, there really is no difference between an expiration date and a "best if used by" date. Major bottled water companies such as Evian, Poland Spring, Aquafina, and Perrier, to name some, voluntarily place expiration dates on their containers as a courtesy to customers. The water is still safe to drink after the listed date if the container has retained its seal, according to a Poland Spring spokesperson, but it could exhibit off-flavors or odors if it has not been stored properly. The typical expiration date is two years from the packaging date. Dasani, a Coca-Cola brand, stamps a one-year expiration date on its water. The popular Fiji brand uses a "best if used by" date.

The FDA Center for Food Safety and Applied Nutrition defines "best if used by" as the deadline for consuming a food to assure the best flavor and quality. But if you store your unopened bottled water in a cool place, that date might never truly arrive.

Chapter 5
KEEPING THE FAITH

Q Can anyone buy a Popemobile?

A The pope has it pretty sweet. He sits on a golden throne in a golden palace in the center of his very own city-state. Everywhere he goes, millions of people weep and cheer at the mere sight of him. He's so revered that he can get away with wearing a hat that would get the average guy's ass kicked. But perhaps the sweetest perk of the job is the papal set of wheels, better known as the Popemobile.

For most of the history of Christianity, the pope has been treated like royalty—and transported like royalty, too. For hundreds of years, the pope traveled in a gilded papal carriage. After the advent of automobiles, he began traveling in custom-made vehicles that often included open-air platforms from which he could wave to his beseeching subjects.

After a Turkish gunman shot and wounded John Paul II in 1981, bulletproof glass was installed around the platform. It was around then that the term "Popemobile" came into vogue. (Pope John Paul II requested that people refrain from using the term, believing it undignified. Undignified? Come on, buddy—you're riding in a phone booth.)

Many automakers have produced custom vehicles for the pontiff over the years, though Mercedes-Benz has traditionally built the cars that are used at the Vatican. The pope maintains a fleet of vehicles in the papal garage, but when he globe-trots, he doesn't always have to bring his cars with him. Sometimes, Popemobiles are produced for a single papal visit, as with the one that was designed and built by Francisco Motors in 1995 for John Paul II's visit to the Philippines.

What happens to these vehicles after they have served their purpose? And, more importantly, how can we get one? Theoretically, anyone with enough cash and misplaced desire can pay a car company to custom-produce a Popemobile, but good luck trying to get one that has been retired from service. These vehicles are usually displayed as museum pieces. An exception was the Range Rover that was specially produced for the pope's visit to Scotland in 1982. The twenty-four ton, six-wheel vehicle was put up for auction in 2006 and fetched $70,500.

Sometimes, though, you can find other types of cars that have been used by his holiness. In 2005, a German man sold a pope-related vehicle for about 189,000 euros—almost a quarter of a million dollars—on eBay. It was a Volkswagen Golf that Pope Benedict XVI had driven when he was a cardinal. But that's nothing compared to the $690,000 that a Texas lawyer ponied up for one of John Paul II's old cars at a 2005 auction. What was it? A dented, powder-blue 1975 Ford Escort.

Q Did some popes have children?

A Yes. And lovers. And very few scruples. The first pope to have a child—at least, the first we know of—was Saint Hormisdas in the sixth century. Hormisdas, once a happily married man, heard God's call late in life. His son, Silverius, became pope in 536, thirteen years after his father's reign ended. Today, that would be the basis of a sitcom: My Son, the Pope.

But you're probably more interested in the lewd, salacious adventures of the naughty popes, and there are plenty of those. The worst popes, in terms of morals, ethics, and criminal behavior, held power during the fifteenth and sixteenth centuries. Let's start with Pius II, pope from 1458 to 1464. Always a bit of a rake, he wrote love poems and fathered at least two illegitimate children while traveling on diplomatic missions for the church. Pius II became a priest after turning forty, was a bishop within a year, and pope twelve years later.

Twenty years after Pius II's death, a cardinal with seven illegitimate children assumed the incongruous name Pope Innocent VIII. He is remembered as one of the greediest popes, selling offices to corrupt priests and using the Vatican as the setting for his son's marriage into the powerful Medici family.

Rodrigo Borgia had four children by one married lover and three others by different women when he became Pope Alexander VI in 1492. Two more of his children were born after his election. Alexander set up his married mistress in a suite at the Vatican, where she was privately known as "the bride of Christ."

Rumors handed down through the centuries suggest that the Borgia pope also slept with his daughter Lucrezia. True or not, the pope did leave his daughter in charge of the Vatican when he had to travel, making her, in effect, a female pope. He used the papacy to secure advantageous marriages for his children (including three husbands for Lucrezia alone) as well as powerful political positions for his sons.

Alexander seemed intent on turning the Vatican into a secularized Borgia kingdom. He created high church offices for wealthy and ambitious nobles who paid him back with small fortunes, and his son Cesare led military takeovers in province after province. Together, they seized the titles and land of wealthy families and even plotted to invade Tuscany. Alexander VI's sudden death in 1503 put an end to that scheme. Cesare seized the papal treasury after his father died, but within five years he had lost everything and died in battle.

Alexander VI marked a papal low, but the list of popes with children goes on. Julius II, pope from 1503 to 1513, had three daughters. Paul III (1534–1549) had four kids, possibly more, and he made one of his grandsons and a nephew cardinals. The next pope, Julius III, forced his brother to adopt a teenager reputed to be either Julius's own son or his lover, and then made the youth a cardinal.

Before the sixteenth century ended, a spirit of reform swept Rome, and some popes became downright prudish! Ironically, even one of the reformist popes, Gregory VIII, had an illegitimate son. Seems that some habits die hard.

Q Do atheists have to swear on the Bible in court?

A Technically, atheists do not have to swear on the Bible in court. The same goes for agnostics, Buddhists, Gothics, Mormons, Jews, Quakers, Wiccans, Muslims, or any Christian who decides to step out of line. Come on, it *could* happen. Not one single citizen of the United States, no matter what his or her religion, has to swear on the Bible when taking the oath in court, thanks to a Supreme Court ruling saying that the "government may not require a person to swear to any belief he or she does not hold. Witnesses have the option of affirming that they will tell the truth, without reference to the Bible or God."

Where exactly did this Bible-God-oath tradition come from? The word "oath" is Anglo-Saxon in origin, and its meaning is pretty straightforward. An oath is defined as a solemn promise, words of promise, or a swear word. Swearing on the Bible was traditional back in England, where witnesses swore before God—and actually kissed the Bible. But it is important to note that until around the mid-seventeenth century, only Christians had any standing in court. Atheists and those who didn't believe that God punished wrongdoers were disqualified from acting as witnesses under the common law rule.

This is where the word technically comes into play. Back in the seventeenth century, atheists and nonbelievers could be legally disqualified from acting as witnesses under the common law rule. Today, it is against the law to disqualify an atheist from acting as a witness, but it is no secret that he or she can be disqualified in the minds of judges and jurors.

So no, atheists do not have to swear on the Bible in court. They can affirm instead by simply answering "yes" to the following question: "You do affirm that all the testimony you are about to give in the case now before the court will be the truth, the whole truth, and nothing but the truth; this you do affirm under the pains and penalties of perjury?" But doing so in the United States, which has the largest Christian population on the earth (78.5 percent), will probably raise more than just an eyebrow.

Q Do Buddhists consider Buddha a god?

A Like Jesus, Buddha was a religious leader who taught disciples spiritual principles and a new way of life. But while Christians view Jesus as the son of God, Buddhists regard Buddha as a human—an incredibly awesome human, but a human nonetheless.

"Buddha" can be a general term meaning "enlightened one," a person who sees existence as it really is. But when people say "Buddha," they usually mean a specific person, Siddhartha Gautama. He was born in Nepal around 563 BC, and his teachings are the origin of Buddhism.

As with any religious figure that lived long ago, historians disagree on the details of Buddha's life. But the general Buddhist belief goes like this: Siddhartha Gautama was the son of a feudal lord and grew up in sheltered luxury. At twenty-nine, after seeing how others suffered, he left his family and devoted himself to understanding the true nature of life. At thirty-five, after years as a homeless ascetic, he sat under a tree and vowed to stay there until he understood the universe. As he meditated, he saw his many past lives and understood the nature of samsara—a cycle of reincarnation that is determined by karma, the positive and negative actions taken in each life. He also saw how to move beyond this cycle of suffering to a higher plain of existence, called nirvana. He dedicated his life to teaching others dharma, the way to achieve enlightenment.

Buddha communicated his core message through four basic truths:

• Life is suffering.

• This suffering comes from ignorance of the true nature of life.

• To end the suffering, a person must overcome this ignorance and all attachments to earthly things.

• A person can do this by following the noble eightfold path, generally translated as right views, right intention, right speech, right action, right livelihood, right effort, right mindedness, and right contemplation. (Buddha elaborated on each of the eight paths, but for that, we'd need an entire book.)

Buddhists believe that anyone may achieve nirvana, but the expectation is that only Buddhist monks are in the right position to do so. So Buddhists strive to make progress toward achieving enlightenment in a later life. In some schools of thought, anyone who achieves enlightenment is known as a Buddha; in others, only someone who arrived at nirvana without any guidance is called a Buddha, like Gautama and the Buddhas who came before him.

Buddhists believe that when Buddha died, he achieved parinirvana, the final release from the earthly realm. While this is seen as a transition to a higher state of being, it's very different from the concept of a god, since a Buddha did not create the universe and doesn't control it.

If you want to know what the higher state is all about, you'll have to find out the hard way. Better get cracking on that good karma.

Q Do libraries put the Bible in the fiction or nonfiction section?

A Walk into just about any library in the United States and ask for a copy of the Bible. Without hesitation, the librarian will point to the reference section and say, "It's under *B*." Most libraries do not place the Bible in the fiction *or* nonfiction section—the Bible is typically considered adult reference or just plain reference material.

There are exceptions. If a library has more than one copy of the Bible, it will place one in reference and the extras in nonfiction, where patrons can check them out. (Reference materials can't be checked out of any library. The Bible has a permanent place in the reference section because it is considered a heavily used book, much like its neighbor the encyclopedia.)

That said, there is a system for classifying the Bible that's not based on how many copies a specific library branch may have. Like all other books, the Bible has a permanent place in the Dewey Decimal Classification System (DDC), a widely used method for classifying books. The Bible is listed in the DDC religion section, which covers

nine topics, beginning with natural theology and ending with comparative religions.

There you have it. We've just saved you from getting lost the next time you go to your friendly neighborhood library in search of the Bible. Kudos to us.

Q What does the "H" stand for in Jesus H. Christ?

A No religion is filled with more arguments, defenses, explanations, proofs, axioms, theorems, and treatises than Christianity. For hundreds of years, the Western world's greatest philosophical and theological minds have wrestled with such soul-saving questions as the nature of the Trinity and the fate of a stillborn's soul. Untold numbers of scholars, millions of pages, and billions of words have been devoted to the explication and illumination of the spiritual fate of humanity.

Yet there is one question that remains unanswered. It is so weighty and so monumental that none of the greatest theological minds in history—not Saint Augustine, not Thomas Aquinas, not Martin Luther—have had the skill or courage to even broach it. This question, of course, is: What does the "H" stand for in Jesus H. Christ?

Fortunately, we're here to answer the truly important questions in life. "Jesus H. Christ," as most of us know firsthand, is a mild expletive. The phrase is rather versatile—it's handy in moments of frustration, anger, astonishment, and bemusement—and the "H" adds a whimsical touch.

134 • Who What Where When

Where this oath comes from, though, is a matter of debate. Although the phrase seems somewhat modern in sensibility (and, in fact, didn't first appear in print until the late nineteenth century), no less an authority on language than Mark Twain said that Jesus H. Christ was already well established by 1850. Various explanations for the origin of the "H" have been proffered. Logic dictates that the "H" would stand for "holy" or "hallowed" (as in, "Our Father, who art in heaven, hallowed be thy name..."), but logic and Christianity don't always go hand in hand.

Most language scholars believe the "H" is the result of a misunderstanding of the Greek abbreviation for Jesus's name. The word for Jesus in Greek is *Iesous,* and in many Greek artifacts, this name was shortened to the abbreviation *iota, eta, sigma, IES.* The capital letter form of the Greek letter *eta* resembles the Roman capital letter *H,* and so the average person who was used to the Roman alphabet would have been forgiven if he or she mistakenly believed that the middle letter was indeed *H.*

Of course, we are about as morally pure a group as you'll ever find, which is why we never take the good Lord's name in vain. This is another, rarely discussed benefit of the middle initial: Since Jesus Christ doesn't really have a middle name, saying "Jesus H. Christ" doesn't *technically* count as taking the Lord's name in vain. And we're working on a six-thousand-page apologia to prove it.

Q Why do priests wear white collars?

A It seems we've stumbled upon one of the hot topics in the clerical blogosphere. (Who even knew there was a clerical blogosphere?) It's actually not just Catholic priests who sport these circular signifiers, but also pastors in the Lutheran, Episcopal, Anglican, and some other Christian and Pentecostal churches. There's even the odd Buddhist or Baptist who puts one on. The debate centers on how lay society reacts to this white collar. Some men—and women—of the cloth say it is a well-known symbol of holiness that makes them more approachable; others contend that it connotes a certain formality and rigidity that has just the opposite effect.

Either way, the white collar is a remaining portion of what was once a more extensive ensemble. In the earliest days, the business of the church was probably conducted in regular day-to-day clothing. The idea that clergy should wear special garments separating them from secular life seems to have emerged in the fourth century, around the time the Emperor Constantine converted to Christianity and brought the Roman Empire with him. Since then, those performing sacraments and leading Mass have worn liturgical vestments.

In the Middle Ages, to keep the clergy from succumbing to extravagance and to make them easily identifiable outside the walls of the sanctuary, popes instructed priests to dress modestly and simply, usually in a plain black tunic or a cassock. The ensuing years saw other popes exert their influence on priestly fashion, as well. In 1589, for instance, Pope Sixtus V prescribed penalties for priests who failed to wear cassocks. Clement XI loosened things up a bit in 1708, authorizing a shorter, more convenient travel jacket for priests to wear on the road. Seventeen years later, Pope Benedict XIII put his holy foot down and nixed civilian attire altogether.

The Code of Canon Law, which lays out the rules of the Catholic Church, notes that "clerics are to wear suitable ecclesiastical garb according to the norms issued by the conference of bishops and according to legitimate local customs." The trademark component of this ecclesiastical garb is the white collar. One colorful version of the origin of the Roman collar suggests that the slick, detachable number worn today was invented in the late eighteen hundreds by the Scottish—and non-Catholic—Rev. Dr. Donald McLeod. But the inspiration likely came from the Catholic Church's Roman collarino, which had evolved in the sixteen hundreds as a means for priests to keep their black cassock collars clean and also mimicked a popular folded-collar style. A narrow band of linen covered the neckband and could be removed for laundering as needed. So practical! Now sure, white shows dirt more readily than black, but the collar also symbolizes obedience to God, so its pure whiteness—not to mention the challenge of keeping it that way—enhanced the overall effect.

Given the strides we've made with laundering techniques in the past few centuries, those currently encased in the collar report that its purpose has more to do with helping the wearers remember their service and responsibilities, and reminding the lay population that God is present in the world. As Rev. Antonio Hernández, an American Buddhist priest who wears the collar, says, "One has no choice but to guard one's behavior while strapped into one of these."

Q Why does the pope change his name when he takes office?

A Think of it as a safety measure to ensure that the papacy remains classy. The tradition started in the year 533: The Catholic Church had just selected a new pope whose given name was Mercurius, a reference to Mercury, the Roman god of commerce. After centuries of stamping out paganism, having a pope named after a pagan god wouldn't do. So Mercurius became John II.

Over the next several centuries, a few other popes changed their names, but these were exceptions rather than the rule. It wasn't until the year 1009 that name changing became the "in" thing. That's when a pope was chosen who had an unfortunate name: Pietro Osporci. His first name just wouldn't work, since it was derived from Saint Peter, Prince of Apostles and Pontiff *Numero Uno.* (No pope has ever taken this name, because none would compare himself to Saint Peter.) Even worse, Osporci means "pig's snout," so that was no good, either. He chose a more dignified moniker, Sergius IV, and changing names was established as a standard practice. Since then, only two popes—Hadrian VI and Marcellus II, both in the sixteenth century—have kept their birth names.

The practice of taking on a new name can have a spiritual dimension as well. In the Old Testament, for example, an angel defeats Jacob in a wrestling match, demonstrating the sovereignty of God; he then gives Jacob the name Israel, meaning "God commands." And the New Testament tells the story of a man named Simon whom Jesus renamed Peter (and who eventually became Saint Peter) when he became a disciple. In this way, a name change can signify the beginning of a new spiritual life, often in an elevated position.

And what position could be more elevated than the pope's? This may be why renaming is one of the first orders of business after a new pope is selected. As soon as the elected pope accepts the position, the Dean of the College of Cardinals asks him, *"Quomodo vis vocari?"* ("By what name do you wish to be called?")

There's no *Big Book of Pope Names* to consult, but new popes generally name themselves after their predecessors or saints they hope to emulate. For example, Pope Benedict XVI said this about his choice: "Firstly, I remember Pope Benedict XV, that courageous prophet of peace, who guided the Church through turbulent times of war. In his footsteps, I place my ministry in the service of reconciliation and harmony between peoples. Additionally, I recall Saint Benedict of Nursia, co-patron of Europe, whose life evokes the Christian roots of Europe. I ask him to help us all to hold firm to the centrality of Christ in our Christian life: May Christ always take first place in our thoughts and actions."

The name may not be as cool as Pope Awesome the First, but it has a nice ring to it.

Chapter 6
LAW AND DISORDER

Q What are legal ways to dispose of a body?

A Grandpa's gone, and for some people, the most pressing issue is whether to request a pillow in his coffin. For others, the question is not whether Gramps needs head support, but whether his earthly remains should be buried, cremated, frozen, or perhaps, in the not-too-distant future, liquefied.

Humans are the only creatures known to bury their dead in a systematic way. It's a practice that could date back some hundred thousand years or more, and today's most commonly legal method of burial involves a casket. In the United States, about 80 percent of the deceased are laid in a casket and buried. More than half are displayed in an open casket prior to burial; the rest bow out with the lid shut.

Cremation is the second-most popular method of disposal. Cremation reduces the average-size adult to eight pounds of ash and fragments. The remains typically are kept by loved ones in a small container or scattered in a location of special significance to the deceased. The ashes of *Star Trek* creator Gene Roddenberry, for example, were dispersed in outer space.

Cryonic suspension is another legal way to go, though it is far less common than burial or cremation. Also known as solid-state hypothermia, cryonic suspension involves freezing and maintaining a human body in the hope that scientific advances someday will make it possible to resuscitate the deceased. The corpse is frozen and stored at −321 degrees Fahrenheit, which is the boiling point of liquid nitrogen. Going the frozen route requires lots of cold cash: Cryopreservation can cost as much as $150,000, depending on the level of services one selects. Baseball great Ted Williams awaits his next turn at bat at a cryonic facility in Scottsdale, Arizona.

The volunteering of corpses for organ donation or for medical or scientific research is also gaining popularity. It's the only way that many people ever get into medical school.

Alkaline hydrolysis might be the future of legal body disposal. The process involves placing a body in a steel chamber that contains lye that is heated to three hundred degrees Fahrenheit and is pressurized to sixty pounds per square inch. Think of it as being boiled in acid. The remains are a liquid that can be poured down a drain. Alkaline hydrolysis is currently performed only in a couple of research hospitals in the United States, but there is growing support to make this environmentally friendly method of body disposal available through funeral homes.

As for illegal ways to get rid of a body, you need neither scientists nor undertakers. Guys with names like Big Nicky are the experts in this field; cross them or their cronies, and a body might end up "sleeping with the fishes."

Q How can celebrity tabloids get away with publishing obviously untrue stories?

A Supermarket tabloids thrive on publishing outlandish celebrity rumors and innuendo. You'd think that the subjects of their articles would be suing them all the time. How in the world could the tabloids survive the legal fees and multimillion-dollar judgments? The truth is, if tabloids are good at one thing, it's surviving.

There are two kinds of tabloids: the ridiculous that publish stories no one really believes ("Bigfoot Cured My Arthritis!") and those that focus on celebrity gossip.

The ridiculous stories are easy to get away with. They're mostly fabricated or based on slender truths. As long as they contain nothing damaging about a real person, there's no one to file a lawsuit. Bigfoot isn't litigious.

Celebrity gossip is trickier. To understand how tabloids avoid legal problems, we need to learn a little bit about the legal definition of libel. To be found guilty of libel, you must have published something about another person that is provably false.

Moreover, the falsehood has to have caused that person some kind of damage, even if only his or her reputation is harmed. If the subject of the story is a notable person, such as a politician or a movie star, libel legally occurs only if publication of the falsehood was malicious. This means that the publisher knew the information was false, had access to the truth but ignored it, and published the information anyway.

Tabloids generally have lawyers on staff or on retainer who are experts in media law and libel. By consulting with their lawyers, tabloid editors can publish stories that get dangerously close to libel but don't quite cross the line.

One defense against libel is publication of the truth: You can't sue someone for saying something about you that's true, no matter how embarrassing it may be. And tabloids know that if they print something close to the truth, a celebrity is unlikely to sue because a trial could reveal a skeleton in the closet that's even more embarrassing.

Libel lawyers also know that a tabloid is in the clear if it publishes a story based on an informant's opinion. Opinions can't be disproved, so they don't meet the criteria for libel. This explains headlines such as this: "Former Housekeeper Says Movie Star Joe Smith Is a Raving Lunatic!" As long as the tabloid makes a token effort to corroborate the story—or even includes a rebuttal of the housekeeper's claims within the article—it is fairly safe from a legal standpoint.

Of course, legal tricks don't always work. Some movie stars, musicians, and other celebrities have successfully sued tabloids for tens of millions of dollars. That tabloids continue to thrive despite such judgments shows just how much money there is to be made in the rumors-and-innuendo business.

Q Are there secret agents like James Bond who are licensed to kill?

A It would seem so, but they're not living the life of James Bond. The concept of "license to kill" wouldn't have such popular resonance without Ian Fleming's James Bond novels and short stories, which have been turned into popular movies for decades. Bond is an agent of MI6—the British Secret Intelligence Service—and his "00" license affords him a wide berth to commit whatever acts, romantic or deadly, he deems fit in order to save humankind. Bond's enemies, after all, make no small plans.

In real life, "license to kill" appears to be more of an implication of broad, nebulous powers granted by heads of state to intelligence agencies and military branches, usually in wartime and often restricted by various legal authorities. That's not to say that agents can't kill with some impunity; they just can't be as swashbuckling as Bond.

For instance, within the British Intelligence Services Act, the Secretary of State can give an agent authority to commit acts abroad without being held accountable under British law. Because killing is not specifically forbidden, it is thus allowed. However, the Act does not absolve the agent of guilt within the foreign country where a killing takes place, because it can't. Hence the "secret" part of "secret agent."

The online magazine *Slate* notes that no MI6 officer has ever publicly admitted to or been charged by an enemy state with killing an enemy, but it's believed that assassinations did take place during World War II and the Cold War. These were committed by British Special Forces, or "foreign third parties," *Slate* says.

A broad kind of license was granted to the CIA soon after 9/11, in a secret document signed by President George W. Bush that directed the CIA to kill al-Qaeda members covertly anywhere in the world. The document did not exclude Americans from being among potential targets, an omission that loomed large when, on November 3, 2002, a missile from a remotely piloted CIA plane blew up a car in Yemen that was carrying the top al-Qaeda operative in that country, other suspected al-Qaeda members, and a U.S. citizen who was only later alleged to have been a cell leader in Buffalo, New York, but who had not been accused of any crime in the United States.

This caused some outrage in the United States, but the Bush administration had the advantage of popular support for the "war on terror" and a lack of clear legality regarding how far the president can extend his wartime authority to order the killing of enemy soldiers. Administrations take advantage of this vagueness. Reportedly in 2003, Donald Rumsfeld's United States Defense Department issued a secret directive ordering the Commander of Special Operations (Green Berets, Delta Force, Navy Seals, the 75th Ranger Regiment, and others) to "develop a plan . . . to capture terrorists for interrogation or, if necessary, to kill them, not simply to arrest them in a law-enforcement exercise," according to *The New Yorker.*

Fleming conceived his James Bond in a time of "noble" wars that lived in the public imagination differently than today's morally complex wars do. Thus, his Bond was endowed with a kind of outsized heroism and simplicity of purpose that is nothing like the current reality. Today's "secret agents" operate within the gray areas of the law, during wars not always formally declared. It's pretty certain that somewhere on the globe there is a U.S. agent with

sufficient legal leeway to kill whom he wants, when he wants—
or, more likely, whom his government tells him—outside of the
traditional context of a declared war. But the U.S. government isn't
going to make a movie out of it. And besides, we hear that Roger
Moore wouldn't be interested in the role.

Q Can a criminal collect a reward on himself?

A It's highly unlikely, but not impossible. Anyone can offer a
reward: the family of a crime victim, a concerned citizens'
group, a corporation, and a nonprofit organization such as
Crime Stoppers, which pays for anonymous tips. And some
local government bodies even offer rewards in certain criminal
investigations. But there are no uniform laws or regulations
regarding how these rewards are disbursed.

In point of fact, whoever offers the reward gets to decide who can
collect the money. Nonetheless, it's difficult to imagine a provision
that would allow the perpetrator of the crime to pocket the dough.

The business of rewards can be tricky. A well-publicized, big-money
offer sometimes works against an investigation by attracting greedy
tipsters who provide useless leads to overworked detectives. Law
enforcement agencies generally don't discourage
reward offers, but they do try to use them
strategically. Often they won't publicize
a reward until an investigation nears
a dead end, the hope being that it'll
renew interest in the crime and jog the
memories of legitimate tipsters.

Many police officials concede that offers of a reward rarely lead to a successful investigation. Most useful tips, they say, come from honest citizens with good intentions that go beyond recompense.

And the existence of a reward doesn't necessarily mean the tipsters will know how to collect it. In July 2008, the FBI offered a twenty-five-thousand-dollar reward in its search for Nicholas Sheley, a suspect in a series of killings. Sheley, it seems, walked into a bar in Granite City, Illinois, to get a drink of water. The bar's patrons had seen his face on the TV news. One called the police; another ran outside and flagged down a squad car. Sheley was quickly taken into custody. Four months later, an FBI spokesman said that nobody had stepped forward to collect the twenty-five grand.

Never mind the bad guys. Sometimes even the good guys don't get the money.

Q Do prisoners still make license plates?

A If you live and drive in the United States, there's a good chance that your car's license plate was made by prison inmates. Forty-seven states, plus the District of Columbia, rely on correctional facilities to manufacture license plates. Only Alaska, Hawaii, and Oregon do not utilize convict labor.

License plates date nearly to the dawn of the automobile. New York was the first state to require them, in 1901, and others soon followed. Each car was assigned a number, and its owner was expected to make the license plate. Not surprisingly, this led to a variety of strange and interesting designs. Most plates were fashioned from wood, leather, or porcelain. For years, Sears,

Roebuck and Co. offered a license-plate design kit in its mail-order catalog. Massachusetts began issuing standardized plates in 1903, and within fifteen years, every state had followed suit.

The link between prisons and plates has its roots in a movement in the late nineteen hundreds toward more benevolent treatment of the incarcerated. It produced reforms that mandated inmates be given useful, productive work.

Pennsylvania was the first state to have prisoners make license plates. In 1920, John R. Wald, superintendent of the state's Prison Labor Division, invented a die machine for stamping letters and numbers on metal plates. He installed it in the Huntington Reformatory; by 1924, Huntington inmates were producing eleven thousand license plates a day. Other state prison systems quickly instituted similar programs.

Plate-making prisoners have adapted to new technology over the years. The Digital License Plate system, developed by technology giant 3M, enables individuals and groups to develop custom license-plate designs on a computer. Prison officials initially feared the software would put them out of the license-plate business, but inmates proved to be adept with the high-tech tools. Some states take orders for plates from all over the world.

Inmates today make everything from sneakers to circuit boards. Some work as call-center representatives, filling merchandise orders and booking hotel rooms. But regardless of whatever else they do, prisoners will always be best known for license plates. And for many of these inmates, the license plates that they produce are their only connections to the glorious freedom of the open road.

Q How crazy do you have to be to be considered legally insane?

A No, judges don't keep a "You must be *this* nuts to get out of jail" sign hidden behind their benches. But you can be found not guilty by reason of insanity if you're cuckoo in just the right way.

Criminal insanity doesn't refer to any specific mental disorder, but it is related to mental illness. The reasoning behind the insanity defense is that some mental disorders may cause people to lose the ability to understand their actions or to differentiate between right and wrong, leaving them unable to truly have criminal intent. Intent is an important element of crime. If you *intentionally* burn down a house by dropping a lit cigarette in a trash can, we'd call you an arsonist. But if you do exactly the same thing accidentally, we'd probably just call you an inconsiderate (and perhaps a criminally negligent) jerk.

Similarly, the reasoning goes, you shouldn't be punished if a mental illness leads you to break the law without really comprehending your actions. Now, this doesn't apply to just any run-of-the-mill murderer with an antisocial personality disorder. A lack of empathy may lead someone to commit crimes, but if he understands what he's doing and he realizes that what he's doing is wrong, he's not insane.

You can only be found not guilty by reason of insanity in two cases: if mental illness keeps you from understanding your actions and deprives you of the ability to tell right from wrong, or if mental illness leaves you unable to control your actions and you experience an irresistible impulse to commit a crime. Details vary from state to state (and some states don't recognize the insanity defense at all), but these are the general criteria.

Some form of the insanity defense seems to date back to the sixteenth century, but early versions were awfully hazy. The 1843 trial of Daniel M'Naghten helped to clear things up. Thinking that the pope and English Prime Minister Robert Peel were out to get him, M'Naghten went to 10 Downing Street to kill Peel but ended up killing Peel's secretary. Witnesses claimed that M'Naghten was delusional, and the jury found him not guilty by reason of insanity. Queen Victoria was none too pleased, so a panel of judges was convened to clarify the rules governing the insanity defense as it involved the inability to distinguish right from wrong.

The definition has been controversial ever since, and every high-profile case seems to throw the idea into question. Patty Hearst and Jeffery Dahmer both tried to use the insanity defense unsuccessfully, while David Berkowitz (Son of Sam) and Ted Kaczynski (the Unabomber) seemed ready to pursue the defense but ultimately decided against it. But a jury did acquit John Hinckley Jr. of all charges related to his assassination attempt on President Reagan after it determined that he was insane.

A successful insanity plea is rare. In the 1990s, a study funded by the National Institute of Mental Health found that defendants pleaded insanity in less than 1 percent of cases, and that only a quarter of those pleas were successful. Those who are successful hardly ever get off scot-free. They're simply committed to mental institutions rather than sent to prisons; on average, those who are found insane end up spending more time confined to an institution than they would have in prison if they had been found guilty.

So unless you really love padded rooms, it's probably best to try another defense.

Q How do you make a citizen's arrest?

A Nearly every state allows an ordinary person to make a citizen's arrest, but this doesn't mean that you should convert your garage into a jail and start rounding up suspected criminals. Perp-busting is best left to professionals.

The concept of a citizen's arrest dates to medieval England, where it was standard practice for ordinary people to help maintain order by apprehending and detaining anyone who was observed committing a crime. This remained part of English common law and, over the years, the concept spread to other countries. Standards of exactly what citizens could and couldn't do to detain suspected criminals were modified over the years, as well.

Today, laws governing citizen's arrests vary from country to country; in the U.S., they vary from state to state. The intent is to give citizens the power to stop someone from inflicting harm when there's no time to wait for authorities. It's considered a last resort and is only meant for dire emergencies.

Every state except North Carolina explicitly grants citizens (and, generally, other residents) the power to arrest someone who is seen committing a felony. Some states extend this to allow a citizen's arrest when the citizen has probable cause to believe that someone has committed a felony.

"Arrest" in this context means stopping and detaining the suspect until law enforcement arrives. Kentucky law kicks it up a notch—it grants citizens the right to use deadly force to stop a fleeing suspected felon.

The general guidelines for a citizen's arrest in the United States break down like this: In most cases, you can arrest someone during or immediately following the commission of a criminal act. First, you tell the suspect to stop what he or she is doing, and then you announce that you're making a citizen's arrest. As long as the suspect stays put, you don't have the right to physically restrain him or her.

Don't notify the suspect of his or her constitutional rights; this would be considered impersonating an officer. Typically, you don't have the right to search or interrogate a suspect, either. If the suspect resists, you have the right to use enough force to detain him or her until law enforcement arrives. It's illegal to use excessive force or to imprison someone extendedly if either is due to your failure to notify law enforcement immediately.

Even if you follow the law to the letter, making a citizen's arrest is risky business because, among other reasons, the law doesn't grant you the same legal protection it gives a police officer. In most cases, the suspect could sue you personally for false arrest or false imprisonment, especially if he or she ends up being acquitted of the charges. In other words, if you see a fishy-looking character running down the street, think twice before you spring into action and yell, "Stop!"

Q What's the difference between a copyright, a patent, and a trademark?

A Think of it this way: You patent your design for self-cleaning underpants, you trademark the name TidyWhities, and you copyright your TidyWhities spin-off cartoon.

The difference between copyrights, patents, and trademarks is that each protects a different type of intellectual property. Normally when we think of property, we think of houses or cars or pieces of land—things that exist in the physical world. A piece of intellectual property, on the other hand, is a product of the mind, like a song or a slogan or an invention. And in order to encourage innovation, our laws protect this kind of property, as well. After all, why would you bother putting in the countless hours of R&D necessary to perfect your TidyWhities if you knew that Hanes could swoop in and rip off your design whenever it wanted?

Copyrights cover what the law calls "original works of authorship" —any unique and tangible creation. As soon as you paint a picture, write a song, film a movie, scribble out a blog post, etc., it's automatically copyrighted. (Although it's a good idea to stamp your masterwork with the copyright symbol, your name, and the year, just to stake your claim.) You can register copyrighted works with the U.S. Copyright Office to firmly establish your authorship, but the copyright exists whether you do this or not.

It's important to remember that copyrights only apply to the form of the creation, not to any of the information that it may contain. For example, the facts in this book are not subject to copyright. But the way in which we've woven these facts together to create a stunning tapestry of knowledge is totally copyrighted, dude. (Bootleggers, get to steppin'.) If you create something and copyright it yourself, the protection lasts for your lifetime plus seventy years.

Unlike a copyright, which covers the material form of an idea, a patent covers an idea itself. It can't be just any brainwave, though; only ideas for inventions and designs can be patented. The most common type of patent protection is the utility patent, which applies to ideas for machines, processes (like a manufacturing process), compositions of matter (like a new fabric), and new uses for any of these things.

Another difference between patents and copyrights is that patents aren't granted automatically. To get one, you have to file an application with the U.S. Patent and Trademark Office, including a thorough written description of your idea, typically with supporting diagrams. Patent examiners review every application to determine if its idea is sufficiently different from previous inventions, actually doable (no time-machine concepts, please), and "non-obvious." The non-obvious requirement prevents inventors from patenting easy tweaks to existing inventions (making a giant spatula, for example).

Although the utility patent is the most commonly issued type of patent protection, there are others worth noting. Plant patents are similar, but cover original plant species that are engineered by humans. Design patents, on the other hand, cover only non-functional designs for products (the exact shape of your TidyWhities, for example).

When a patent is approved, the inventor has the legal right to stop others from making or selling the invention for a period of twenty years. The inventor can make money by selling the invention exclusively or by licensing the idea to a company that can manufacture and market the product.

This brings us to the trademark. This is the narrowest form of intellectual property protection—it covers names and symbols that indicate the source of a product or service. For example, Apple has trademarked its little apple icon, as well as the words "Apple" and "Macintosh" when applied to computers and electronics. When the U.S. Patent and Trademark Office grants you a trademark, it remains yours for as long as you keep using the name or symbol. Hmm, wonder if TidyWhities is taken.

Q What's the difference between a mass murderer and a serial killer?

A Serial killers are made of sugar and spice and everything nice, and mass murderers are...wait, that's not right. The distinction is actually very simple.

A mass murderer kills four or more people during a short period of time, usually in one location. In most cases, the murderer has a sudden mental collapse and goes on a rampage, progressing from murder to murder without a break. About half the time, these outbreaks end in suicides or fatal standoffs with the police. Various school shootings over the years have been instances of mass murder, as have been famous cases of postal workers, well, "going postal." A case in which someone murders his or her entire family is a mass murder. Terrorists are lumped into this category as well, but they also make up a group of their own.

A serial killer usually murders one person at a time (typically a stranger), with a "cooling off" period between each transgression.

Unlike mass murderers, serial killers don't suddenly snap one day—they have an ongoing compulsion (usually with a sexual component) that drives them to kill, often in very specific ways. They may even maintain jobs and normal relationships while going to great lengths to conceal their killings. They may resist the urge to kill for long periods, but the compulsion ultimately grows too strong to subjugate. After the third victim, an aspiring killer graduates from plain ol' murderer to bona fide serial killer.

In between these two groups, we have the spree killer and the serial spree killer. A spree killer commits murder in multiple locations over the course of a few days. This is often part of a general crime wave. For example, an escaped convict may kill multiple people, steal cars, jaywalk, and litter as he tries to escape the police. As with a mass murderer, a spree killer doesn't plan each murder individually.

The serial spree killer, on the other hand, plans and commits each murder separately, serial-killer style. But he or she doesn't take time off between murders or maintain a double life. It's all killing, all the time. One of the best-known examples is the Washington, D.C.-area beltway snipers who killed ten people within three weeks in October 2002.

Of course, if you see any of these types of killer in action, don't worry about remembering the right term when you call the police. They're all equally bad.

Q Whose bright idea was it to electrocute criminals?

A Dr. Alfred Southwick. Southwick was a dentist in Buffalo, New York, but he was no simple tooth-driller. Like many of his contemporaries in the Gilded Age of the 1870s and 1880s, he was a broad-minded man who kept abreast of the remarkable scientific developments of the day—like electricity. Though the phenomenon of electric current had been known of for some time, the technology of electricity was fresh—lightbulbs and other electric inventions had begun to be mass produced, and the infrastructure that brought electricity into the businesses and homes of the well-to-do was appearing in the largest cities.

So Southwick's ears perked up when he heard about a terrible accident involving this strange new technology. A man had walked up to one of Buffalo's recently installed generators and decided to see what all the fuss was about. In spite of the protests of the men who were working on the machinery, he touched something he shouldn't have and, to the shock of the onlookers, died instantly. Southwick pondered the situation with a cold, scientific intelligence and wondered if the instant and apparently painless death that high voltage had delivered could be put to good use.

Southwick's interest in electrocution wasn't entirely morbid. Death—or more specifically, execution—was much on people's minds in those days. Popular movements advocated doing away with executions entirely, while more moderate reformers simply wanted   a new, more humane method of putting criminals to death. Hangings had fallen out of favor due to the potential for gruesome accidents, often caused by the incompetence of hangmen. While the hangman's goal was to break the criminal's neck instantly, a loose knot could result in an agonizingly slow suffocation; a knot that was too tight had the potential to rip a criminal's head clean off.

To prove the worth of his idea, Southwick began experimenting on dogs (you don't want to know) and discussing the results with other scientists and inventors. He eventually published his work and attracted enough attention to earn himself an appointment on the Gerry Commission, which was created by the New York State Legislature in 1886 and tasked with finding the most humane method of execution.

Although the three-person commission investigated several alternatives, eventually it settled on electrocution—in part because Southwick had won the support of the most influential inventor of the day, Thomas Alva Edison, who had developed the incandescent lightbulb and was trying to build an empire of generators and wires to supply (and profit from) the juice that made his lightbulbs glow. Edison provided influential confirmation that an electric current could produce instant death; the legislature was convinced and a law that made electrocution the state's official method of execution was passed.

On August 6, 1890—after much technical debate (AC or DC? How many volts?) and a few experiments on animals (again, you don't want to know)—William Kemmler, an axe murderer, became the first convicted criminal to be electrocuted. Southwick declared it a success, but the reporters who witnessed it felt otherwise. Kemmler had remained alive after the first jolt, foam was oozing from the mask that had been paced over his face as he struggled to breathe. A reporter fainted. A second jolt of several minutes was applied, and Kemmler's clothes and body caught fire. The stench of burned flesh was terrible.

Despite a public outcry, the state of New York remained committed to the electric method of execution. The technology and technique were improved, and eventually other states began to use electrocution as well. Today, eight states still allow use of the electric chair, though lethal injection is the preferred option.

Q Why do judges wear black robes?

A Because black is slimming, of course!

If only it were that easy. The real reason judges wear black robes is up for debate, though only slightly. Ask any member of the Catholic Church and he or she will tell you that this practice is purely an ecclesiastical tradition. During the fifteen hundreds, priests wore black robes. And during this time, priests were—you guessed it— judges, too.

But black wasn't the end-all back then. English court dress was quite flamboyant, to say the least. Judges would wear a black robe trimmed in fur during the winter months and a violet or scarlet robe trimmed in pink taffeta during the summer months. No wonder these robes were referred to as "costumes" in the Judges' Rules that were set forth after 1635. Judges also wore black girdles underneath their robes.

Court dress continued to evolve, and accessories were piled onto the already ornate ensemble. By the mid-eighteenth century, judges began to take even more liberties with their costumes. For criminal trials, they wore scarlet robes with a matching hood and a black scarf. For civil trials, many judges kept it simple and wore a black silk gown. After years and years of indecisiveness and plenty of lilac and mauve, most courts settled on the simple black silk gown as a base. Ceremonial occasions were (and still are) an entirely different beast—we're talking silk stockings, leather pumps, and all kinds of shiny buckles. But that's a different story.

Today, the black robe is fairly standard in courtrooms around the world (depending on the court or level). In the good old USA, the black robe is definitely the garb of choice. You will never see a U.S. judge (in open court) decked out in fur trim, bright colors (definitely not pink), and, um, a girdle.

Q Is it okay to marry your cousin?

A It sure is, at least in some parts of the world. Take Saudi Arabia. According to the *New York Times*, the Saudi government reports that 55 to 70 percent of marriages are between blood relatives. In fact, across the Arab world, 45 percent of all married couples are related, according to Dr. Nadia Sakati, a senior consultant for the genetics research center at King Faisal Specialist Hospital in Riyadh, Saudi Arabia.

In Pakistan (where cousin marriage is traditional and arranged) and Indonesia, the thought is that when you marry a family member, you know with whom you are dealing. It also preserves parental control and ensures that any wealth will stay in the family, although this is considered less important.

In China, there are some sixty million girls who would have been viable candidates for marriage if not for gender-based abortions and female infanticide, so a man sometimes has little choice but to marry a close family member (though not if it's his paternal uncle's daughter, as patrilateral parallel cousin marriage is forbidden). In the United States, marrying one's cousin brings up subjects such as incest and inbreeding, and conjures up images of a banjo-playing boy and homosexual hillbillies from the 1970s cult film *Deliverance*.

The taboo attached to consanguineous marriage (cousin marrying) in the United States dates back to the nineteenth century, when westbound settlers wanted to distinguish themselves from Native Americans. Among other things, they proposed that no "white man" marry his cousin, because that is what the "savages" did.

However, anthropologists say that male Native Americans had no need to marry their female kin because there were plenty of other women available. Male European settlers, on the other hand, had fewer non-kin women from which to choose from, and some did marry within their bloodlines.

Not only is marrying your cousin taboo in the United States, it is illegal in some areas. Twenty-four states have laws that make it a crime to marry your first cousin, and five other states permit the union only if the couple is incapable of reproducing. These laws, in most cases, have been on the books for more than a century and are considered outdated, especially when the latest findings on the subject of consanguineous marriages are taken into consideration.

The National Society of Genetic Counselors (NSGC), a leading authority in the field, funded a study that found that children born to first-cousin couples are at only slightly higher risk for genetic disorders such as cystic fibrosis, Tay Sachs, or congenital heart defects. The offspring of a "normal" couple have a 3 to 4 percent chance of having these defects, and children of a first-cousin couple have an increased risk of only 1.7 to 2.8 percent.

The offspring of second cousins who marry are in the normal range for birth defects. Based on the NSGC's findings, which involved the review of six major studies conducted from 1965 to 2000 that involved several thousand births, the organization concluded that there is no biological reason for first cousins not to marry.

This would be a relief to some famous persons who married their first cousins: Queen Victoria, Edgar Allan Poe, Charles Darwin, Jesse James, and H. G. Wells. Not enough star power for you in that group? Okay, then you might want to consult the 1913 *Catholic Encyclopedia*, which contains an entry speculating that Mary and Joseph, the mother and father of Jesus, were first cousins.

Q Why does the U.S. government think you need to be twenty-one to buy a beer but only eighteen to buy a gun?

A The United States has some strange laws. In one Illinois town, you can't give a lit cigar to a domesticated animal. In Marshalltown, Iowa, horses are prohibited from eating fire hydrants. In Gary, Indiana, it is illegal to go to a theater or opera house within four hours of eating garlic. (Of course, this would entail finding a theater or opera house in Gary.) But perhaps the most incongruous laws are two that are shared by just about every state: You have to be twenty-one to legally buy a beer, but only eighteen to purchase a lethal weapon.

The history of the United States is filled with moral righteousness. This can largely be traced back to the Puritans who came over from England seeking to build their morally perfect "city on a hill." The influence of these dour settlers has resonated for centuries in the form of highly restrictive legal codes, like the ill-advised experiment with Prohibition in the 1920s and 1930s. When Prohibition was overturned, most state leaders compromised with their teetotaling voters and set the drinking age at twenty-one.

Guns have been subject to much less regulation than alcohol over the course of U.S. history, in part because the founding fathers decided that everyone should have the right to bear one—or at least to carry one while serving in a militia, depending on whom you ask. Indeed, it wasn't until the Gun Control of Act of 1968 that there was even an age limit for purchasing guns by mail—eighteen for rifles and twenty-one for handguns. And as every patriotic red-blooded American knows, you only need to be eighteen to enlist in the United States military.

The legal drinking and gun-owning ages were on a collision course during the Vietnam War, when young Americans who had been, drafted into a war that many of them didn't want to fight, pointed out that it seemed illogical for the government to trust an eighteen-year-old soldier to handle an M-16 in a foreign land but not a beer at the local tavern. Partially as a result of this, many states experimented with lowering the drinking age, some to as low as eighteen years old.

Makes sense, right? Wrong. In this case, the government had been right in the first place—or so the numbers seem to indicate. Study after study has shown that lowering the drinking age increased alcohol-related traffic accidents. As a result, the brief experiment ended, and today all fifty states require drinkers to be at least twenty-one years old.

Regardless of age limits, guns and alcohol never mix. In 1997, a drunken young Florida man entered a Kmart to purchase a rifle. The fact that he was so drunk that he needed a clerk to help him fill out the paperwork didn't faze store employees. It should have: The man left the store and shot his ex-girlfriend, leaving her paralyzed. But hey, at least he didn't imitate an animal while buying the gun—in Miami, that's against the law.

Chapter 7
LOCATION, LOCATION, LOCATION

Q Did Troy exist?

A Sure. Troy Aikman, Troy Donahue, Troy, Michigan—which one do you want to read about? Oh, you're thinking about Troy, the site of the Trojan War? Yup, that existed too.

If you remember your history classes—or if you saw the movie—you know that Troy was the walled city of the Trojans. Troy's Prince Paris stole the beautiful Helen from her husband in Sparta and carried her back to Troy. The disgruntled husband and all his kingly friends began a war that lasted ten years and ended with Troy's destruction. This was chronicled in *The Iliad,* Europe's oldest epic poem. How old? Perhaps three thousand years old.

The Greeks and Romans never doubted that Troy had been a real place, situated near the Dardanelles—today, a part of Turkey. In 1870, a German-born archaeologist named Heinrich Schliemann announced that he'd discovered the ruins of Troy. Schliemann dug into a mound called Hisarlik and found layers of ancient cities, each built on the ruins of earlier settlements. He found (or possibly faked) gold treasures, but it was his assistant—Wilhelm Dörpfeld—who later realized that no fewer than nine separate cities had been built on that spot. Conveniently, they're labeled Troy I through Troy IX.

Troy I began as a Stone Age village around 3600 BC. Over the millennia, it evolved into a royal city. Schliemann assumed that remains near the bottom of his excavation—Troy II—were from the real Troy, because Troy II was destroyed by fire. *That* fortified city, though, dates back to 2300 BC—far too early to be the Troy of legend. Scholars today believe that *The Iliad*'s Troy is probably Troy VIIa, built on the ruins of a richer city that was destroyed by an earthquake in the twelfth century BC.

How much of *The Iliad* is based on fact? We will probably never know, partly because very little evidence can survive for three thousand years, but mostly because Schliemann's excavation methods destroyed more than they saved.

From 1982 until his death in 2005, German archaeologist Manfred Korfmann made more discoveries near the site of Troy. He found that a fifty-foot-high burial mound, long called the Tomb of Achilles, did indeed date from the time of Troy VIIa. Korfmann also excavated a cemetery with more than fifty Greek graves from the same period. Swords and pottery imply that Greek aristocrats were buried there, along with women and children. What's more, Korfmann may have found the ancient harbor and camp where most of *The Iliad*'s action took place. Although not every scholar and archaeologist accepts this site as ancient Troy, it was declared a UNESCO World Heritage Site in 1998.

Now, about Troy Aikman . . .

Q Where is No Man's Land?

A For a place so desolate, No Man's Land sure has a lot of locations. Take a look at a map and you will find a No Man's Land in the Caradon district of southeast Cornwall, England; a No Man's Land on East Falkland Island; and a Nomans Land Island (also charted No Man's Land or No Man's Island) in Chilmark, Massachusetts. And that's just to name a few.

Some of these places are indeed uninhabited, but that's probably for good reason. In the case of the Falkland Island No Man's Land, the terrain is extremely rough due to a craggy chain of mountains known as Wickham Heights.

And the No Man's Land in Massachusetts? It is located only three miles off the quaint coast of Martha's Vineyard, but this island was once used as a practice range for bombing. It's closed to the public, apparently due to concern about unexploded ordnance that still might detonate.

In more general terms, No Man's Land is a phrase that has been around since at least the fourteenth century. It's often used to reference an unoccupied area between the front lines of opposing armies, or to designate land that is unowned, undesirable, or otherwise under dispute.

A good example: Following the Louisiana Purchase between the United States and Spain, an area called No Man's Land (a.k.a. the Neutral Strip or Sabine Free State) was designated neutral ground because the two governments could not agree on a boundary. From 1806 to 1819, both countries claimed ownership of this tract, but neither enforced any laws or control. No wonder it became a haven for outlaws and renegades.

In its earliest use, No Man's Land likely referred to a plot of land just outside the north walls of London. In the early thirteen hundreds, this No Man's Land was a place where criminals were executed and left out in the open for public view. There goes the neighborhood.

Q Where is the most crowded place on Earth?

A We know what you're thinking: The most crowded place on Earth must be Disneyland on the first day of summer vacation. Or perhaps the Mall of America on the morning after Thanksgiving. Right?

Wrong. Those are anomalies, and while they might seem like hectic places at certain times, there is a section of Hong Kong that has them both beat 365 days a year. It's called Mong Kok, which translates to "flourishing/busy corner." The name is apt because, according to the *Guinness Book of World Records*, Mong Kok is the most densely populated place on the planet.

About two hundred thousand people reside in Mong Kok, an area just slightly larger than half a square mile. That's about seventy square feet per person. Add in the buildings and you've got a district in which it is physically impossible for everyone to be outside at the same time. (By comparison, the Manhattan borough of New York City is home to about 70,600 people per square mile.)

Mong Kok's bustling Golden Mile—a popular stretch of shops, restaurants, and theaters—compounds the crowding issue: A half-million or so tourists routinely jostle for position in the streets. Residents told the *New York Times* that the streets are often completely full, with every inch of pavement covered.

How is it possible to squeeze so many people into such a small area? You build up. Mong Kok is home to an array of high-rise apartment buildings. Families who live in these apartments sometimes rent out rooms to other families. There might be ten or more people in a single apartment—they sleep in two or three rooms and share a small kitchen and a single bathroom. The apartments are so small that people sleep in bunk beds that are three or four tiers high, and they keep their belongings in chests and baskets that are suspended from the ceiling.

Remember Mong Kok the next time you're elbowing your way through a crowded store on Black Friday, trying to secure the season's must-have toy. When you return home and sit at the table for dinner, at least there won't be two other families smiling back at you.

Q Where is the original skid row?

A Fans of 1980s hair bands have been asking this question for nearly two decades. After exploding onto the rock scene in 1989 with an eponymous powerhouse album—featuring such anthems as "Youth Gone Wild" and the quintessential power ballad "I Remember You"—Skid Row vanished from the public eye a few years later. Whatever happened to Sebastian Bach? What about Snake Sabo? Wait, what's that? You're not asking about the rock band? You say that you're interested in where the phrase "skid row" originated? Well, that certainly is disappointing—we'd already put on our acid-washed jeans and thrust our lighters into the air. But we suppose we can answer that question, too.

"Skid row," a term used to describe a section of an urban community that is inhabited by the poor and down-on-their-luck, has been around since the Great Depression. A variation of the phrase goes back even further, to around 1880. In the Pacific Northwest in the late nineteenth century, logging was a booming business, and getting the timber from the remote mountainsides to lumber mills was no easy task, especially in the rainy conditions that companies often had to work.

To facilitate transportation, lumbermen placed timbers—which were known as "skids"—over the unpaved logging trails. They then dragged the felled logs over these timber-covered logging trails, which became known as "skid roads." (Incidentally, two other phrases are spawned from this practice: "on the skids" and "grease the skids.")

Where the first skid road originated is up for debate—a number of Pacific Northwest cities lay claim to it, including Seattle, where a Skid Road still exists—but it wasn't long before the term was used to describe the parts of town where these hardworking lumbermen lived and would gather on their days off to carouse and behave badly. These questionable parts of the city, which were often filled with saloons and houses of ill repute, also drew the unemployed and others who were down on their luck. Over the next few decades, the term skid road morphed into skid row and spread across the country with the tramps and vagabonds who rode boxcars from city to city.

By the Great Depression, millions of Americans had joined the ranks of the down-and-out, and skid rows popped up in cities across the nation. Nowadays, people don't use the phrase quite as often. In fact, you'd be hard-pressed to find somebody who could direct you to skid row in any modern city. Although if you're looking for the members of the once-great band of the same name, it might be a good place to look.

Q Where is the world's worst place to live?

A The worst place to live, much like beauty, is in the eye of the beholder. If you enjoy long hikes in untrammeled countryside, then the megalopolis Tokyo would probably be a bad match for you. Similarly, if you enjoy the rich culture of a big city, a life spent in Maza, North Dakota (2007 population: four), might seem akin to burning in hell. If you wake up each morning to find that your ex has again slashed your car tires and left a flaming sack of solid waste on your doorstep, then the town in which you reside is most likely the worst place in the world to live.

When serious types sit down to make their worst-cities-in-the-world lists, they usually look at quantifiable measures such as pollution or infant mortality rate. *Popular Science* magazine, for instance, placed Pittsburgh, Pennsylvania, on its list of the world's ten worst cities because of its toxic air quality. Sure, the 'Burgh could stand to learn a thing or two about going green, but take in a baseball game at beautiful PNC Park and head over to Primanti Brothers for a pastrami and cheese, and then try to say it's a terrible place to live.

Another factor that many "worst" lists point to is war. Makes sense. The likelihood of getting killed simply by walking out your front door is a flaw that most prospective homeowners would be unable to overlook. Popular choices in this category feature any number of cities in the war-torn Congo and, of course, Baghdad, Iraq. But bad wars can happen to good cities. There have been a number of violent conflicts in Paris, but most people will agree that the City of Lights has rebounded nicely.

If only there was a city that could bring it all together—a city that could take the constant threat of violence, mix in government corruption, and top it off with squalid living conditions. Well, *The Economist* found just such a place. After reviewing 130 world capitals, the magazine declared that Port Moresby, the capital of Papua New Guinea, is the world's worst place to live. Port Moresby has exceptionally high rates of murder and rape, massive unemployment, and no welfare system.

This sounds horrendous, but remember, it was a survey of only world capitals. Surely there's some off-the-map hellhole that makes Port Moresby look like Aspen. We'll keep looking, but in the meantime Port Moresby is the champ.

Q Why is Chicago called the Windy City?

A Chicago has its own special set of reputations. It's known for blue-collar workers, a losing baseball team, corrupt politicians, and heart attack-inducing foods. The city also has its share of nicknames, such as the Second City and the City of Big Shoulders. For most people, though, Chicago is the Windy City. But why?

Any shivering tourist visiting downtown Chicago during the winter could justifiably assume that this nickname is descriptive of the arctic gales that whip off Lake Michigan. Helpful Chicagoans are quick to rectify this apparent misconception. They explain that Chicago is the Windy City not for meteorological reasons, but because of its great tradition of windbag politicians. The exact phrase is said to date back to 1890, when New York and Chicago battled for the right to host the 1893 World's Fair. The bluster from Chicago politicians in support of their city's bid led Charles Dana, editor of *The* (New York) *Sun,* to urge his readers to reject "the nonsensical claims of that windy city."

For many years, this theory was accepted as fact. It was most recently rehashed by writer Erik Larson in his bestselling book about the 1893 World's Fair, *The Devil in the White City.* One minor hitch: There is no published record of such a statement attributed to Dana. According to Barry Popik, an etymologist who has tracked down the origins of many uniquely American nicknames and slang phrases, the nickname Windy City was introduced long before 1890. Popik says that the first recorded use of the nickname can be traced to 1860 and, perhaps not surprisingly, was indeed related to the strong winds that blow off the lake. In fact, according to Popik, Chicago promoted its windy reputation in an effort to sell itself as a resort destination. (Surely this was one of the least-enticing advertising campaigns in tourism history.)

Still, the theory that links the nickname to windbag politicians might have some credence. In the second half of the nineteenth century, Chicago and Cincinnati waged a fierce war of words over which of the two cities should be considered the pearl of the Midwest. (St. Louis wanted to get in on the rivalry, but it was, you know, St. Louis.) As huge numbers of Americans moved west, midwestern cities tried to lure new residents with advertising and braggadocio, a phenomenon known as boosterism.

Chicago and Cincinnati were major hog-slaughtering centers (apparently a big draw in the nineteenth century), and both boasted about their waterfront views. It didn't take long for Cincinnati newspapers to pick up on the double entendre of "windy" with regard to Chicago. Editorials in Cincinnati newspapers hammered away at Chicago's weather and the empty bluster of its boosterism, successfully saddling their rival to the north with the Windy City moniker. At the same time, Cincinnati won a nickname that signified its meatpacking supremacy: Porkopolis. Who's having the last laugh now?

Q Do all countries have military forces?

A Who wants to know? You looking to start some trouble? Okay, we give: There are twenty-one countries that do not have formal forces. Some have components of a military, such as a Coast Guard, while others have relatively large police forces that may dabble in a little national security on the side.

Most countries that do not have sustainable defensive military forces have a "you scratch my back, and I'll get my back scratched" deal with other nations. France, for instance, is responsible for Monaco, and it shares the responsibility of defending Andorra with Spain. Australia and New Zealand would help out Kiribati if needed. New Zealand must consider all requests for military aid by Samoa in accordance with the most sweetly named treaty ever, the Treaty of Friendship (1962). And of course, Italy would probably have something to say to anyone who tried to mess with the Rome-based Vatican City, although Italy and the Vatican do not have a defense treaty because it would violate the Vatican's neutrality.

Beginning in 1951, Iceland had a deal with the United States that had U.S. military forces stationed there until 2006, when they withdrew. While the United States no longer has a physical presence there, Iceland and the United States have signed a Joint Understanding to continue a "bilateral defense relationship." Since Iceland does have a Coast Guard, there are some things Iceland can share with us. In addition to Iceland, the United States is responsible for defending the Marshall Islands, the Federated States of Micronesia, and Palau, since they are official associated states—free entities with political ties to the United States.

Dominica, Grenada, Saint Lucia, and Saint Vincent and the Grenadines do not have official military forces, but they are all protected under the Regional Security System (RSS). The RSS is an agreement among many Caribbean countries to protect one another.

Haiti, Costa Rica, and a few other small countries don't have militaries, but they do have extensive police forces, some of which have paramilitary units. Haiti's military, while disbanded, still exists on paper in its Constitution.

So, while some countries aren't exactly armed to the teeth, it would still require more than a few drunken friends and some slingshots to take them over.

Q How many countries have a neutralist policy?

 Bent on world domination? To an aspiring dictator, neutral countries can look like the low-hanging fruit on the tree of global conquest. They lack offensive military capabilities and they have wishy-washy foreign policies—in other words, they are there for the taking. Or so it would seem. In fact, this whole "neutral" thing is a lot more complicated than it looks.

First of all, there's a difference between being "neutral" and "neutralist." A neutralist country is one that has a policy of nonalignment: When it seems like the whole world is picking sides in an extended conflict, a neutralist country tries to stay out of it.

The neutralist movement goes back to the Cold War, to countries that refused to affiliate with either the Soviet bloc or the Western bloc of nations. India is one of the largest countries that had a neutralist policy—it tried to (ahem) curry favor with the USSR and the USA alike. But a neutralist policy doesn't mean that a country must avoid aggression. Neutralist countries have actually gone to war with each other, like Iran and Iraq did in the early 1980s.

So how many neutralist countries are there? A lot. So many that they have their own international organization, the Non-Aligned Movement (NAM), which represents most of the countries in South America, Africa, and the Middle East. And though the NAM has been called a relic of the Cold War, it's still alive and kicking.

Now, a "neutral" country is something else entirely. Neutrality is a condition that is recognized by the international laws and treaties that govern warfare. According to these agreements, when a war breaks out, disinterested countries can declare themselves neutral. This means that they have certain rights—the warring nations can't enter their territories, for example—as well as the fundamental responsibility to remain neutral by treating the warring nations impartially. Any country can potentially remain neutral during any war, as long as it can maintain that impartiality.

But this idea of limited neutrality doesn't really get to the heart of our question. We're looking for perpetually neutral countries—the Swedens and the Switzerlands of the world. Switzerland, as you may recall, has had guaranteed neutrality since the Congress of Vienna settled Napoleon's hash in 1815, and the Swedes have been neutral since about that time as well. But although Sweden stayed out of the great wars of the twentieth century, its current neutrality is debatable since it's a member of the European Union (EU) and, as such, has a stake in the EU's non-neutral foreign policy.

That leaves the Swiss. But before you start drawing up your marching orders against the soft underbelly of Switzerland, you should get familiar with the phrase "armed neutrality." This means that the Swiss aren't going to roll over for you—they've got a defensive army, or more accurately, a sort of citizen militia. Switzerland also has one of the highest gun-ownership rates in the world. So beware, aspiring dictators: This world-domination thing isn't as easy as it looks.

Q What are the requirements to be a country?

A Considering the amount of time we spend celebrating global diversity, you'd think that we could all agree on some basic facts about the world—like the number of countries that there are. But no—depending on whom you ask, there are as few as 192 or as many as 260.

Part of the problem is that there's no official rulebook that explains exactly what it takes to be a country. And we certainly can't just take any would-be country's word for it—otherwise those gun-toting survivalists in northern Idaho might have a point about seceding from the Union. In fact, if you think about it, it's kind of hard to define what exactly a country is. The word "country" can evoke a landscape, the people who live on it, or the laws that govern them there—and often it conjures all of those things. The concept of countryhood is one of those ideas that we take for granted but struggle to articulate.

Fortunately, the lawyers of the world have got our backs. International laws can work only if the requirements of countryhood are well defined. One influential legal definition of a country is spelled out in the Montevideo Convention on the Rights and Duties of States, a treaty that was signed by North and South American nations in Montevideo, Uruguay, in 1933. In Article I, it says: "The state as a person of international law should possess the following qualifications: (a) a permanent population; (b) a defined territory; (c) government; and (d) capacity to enter into relations with the other states."

Article III of the treaty makes it clear that any group that meets these four requirements has the right to become a country, even if other countries refuse to recognize it as such. This was an innovation. In earlier times, becoming a country was more like joining an exclusive club: You had to impress the most popular members—namely, the nations that dominated the world with their wealth and military power—and convince them to let you in. Their opinion was the only thing that mattered.

But even under the newer egalitarian rules, there's a loophole that keeps the global "country club" more exclusive than it might seem. According to the Montevideo definition, you need to have "the capacity to enter into relations with other states," which effectively means that other states have to agree to enter into relations with you. In other words, you still have to get at least one country to recognize you, even if you fulfill the other requirements for automatic statehood.

So how do established countries decide which hopefuls they choose to recognize? In practice, it often comes down to political expediency. Taiwan, for example, looks like it fulfills all of the requirements of statehood that are laid out by the Montevideo Convention. But many countries—the United States included—haven't recognized Taiwan as an independent state, because the Chinese, who think of Taiwan as part of their own territory, would be royally pissed.

There you have it. In practice, fully recognized countryhood comes down to who you know, just like virtually everything else in this world.

Q Who's the idiot who named a floating hunk of ice Greenland?

A Let's face it: Explorers weren't always the brightest of the bunch. Brave? Yes. Self-reliant? Maybe. But intelligent? Not so much. To be fair, the great explorers of yore were working without reliable maps. Nevertheless, one has to admit that it was boneheaded for Christopher Columbus to think that an island in the Caribbean was India. Or what about the guy who landed on an enormous iceberg and decided to call it Greenland? Talk about a moron.

Greenland, perhaps best known as the largest island that is not a

Ninety percent of the island is covered by an ice cap and smaller glaciers, which means that the place is mostly uninhabitable. Although the northern coasts of Greenland had been settled for thousands of years by Inuit (the same folks who brought you the igloo), the island was largely unknown to Europeans until the late tenth century.

So how did a country that boasts almost no green land get the name Greenland? Theories abound, including the legend that Iceland switched names with Greenland to avoid being invaded by barbarians. (Barbarians were dumb, but not that dumb.) While this explanation borders on preposterous, it's not as far off the mark as you may think.

Many historians believe that Greenland's name may be derived from one of the biggest—and earliest—marketing scams of all time. In the tenth century, a Viking named Erik the Red fled his home of Iceland after committing murder. Erik took the opportunity to explore the islands and lands to the west of Iceland.

Drifting across the Atlantic, Erik eventually came to the rocky coast of an enormous island that was covered in ice. He had an idea: If he couldn't be with his people, then he'd bring his people to him. Though only a sliver of land was actually green, he promptly named the island Greenland, which, according to the Icelandic sagas, was because "men will desire much the more to go there if the land has a good name."

Icelanders, believing the marketing hype, came in droves, settling along the southern coast of Greenland, where they flourished for several hundred years. To be fair to Red, archaeologists believe that the climate was a bit more temperate during the Vikings' heyday. Still, calling this arctic landmass Greenland is a bit like a modern-day housing developer grandly naming its cookie-cutter development Honey Creek, even though the only "creek" nearby is a sewage canal. At any rate, Erik the Red pulled off one heck of a real-estate swindle.

Interestingly, it was Erik the Red's son, Leif Eriksson, who is widely considered to be the first European to visit North America. In the early eleventh century, Leif ventured with a band of explorers across the Atlantic Ocean, where he discovered the cold, wintry islands of what are now Newfoundland and Labrador, Canada. Leif named his new settlement as only the son of Erik the Red could: Wine Land.

Q Why do so many country names end with "-stan"?

A No, there was no Stan the Conqueror running around founding countries in ancient times. The real answer is a lot less exciting. There are "-stan" countries for the same reason there are "-land" countries—*stan* is an old Persian word meaning "place," "land," or "home." As people from ancient Persia (modern-day Iran) spread to different areas of western Asia, they took the suffix with them.

Today, there are seven independent "-stan" nations in central Asia (including some that creep over into Eastern Europe); five were formerly republics of the Soviet Union. There are also three "-stan" republics in the Russian Federation, three "-stan" provinces in Iran, and several historical "-stan" regions in various Asian countries.

Typically, place names formed with "-stan" describe a land in terms of its inhabitants. For example, Afghanistan means "land of the

Afghans." In other cases, "-stan" formations evoke the landscape itself, like the name Dagestan (a Russian republic), which means "land of the mountains."

Pakistan is a recent addition to the "-stan" list. In 1930, the Muslim philosopher Sir Muhammad Iqbal called for a new Muslim state to be carved out of what was then British India. Students who supported the idea proposed calling the new country Pakistan for its double meaning. It literally meant "land of the pure" (pak), and according to Peter Blood's book Pakistan: A Country Study, it also incorporated letters from some of the predominantly Muslim regions in the area—Punjab, Afghania, Kashmir, Iran, Sindh, Tukharistan, Afghanistan, and Balochistan.

Just think—if Persians had discovered the New World, we might all be living in the United States of Americastan.

Chapter 8
MONEY MATTERS

Q **If you have no heirs, who gets all your stuff when you die?**

A While it's true that you can't take it with you, you can, with the help of a will, at least decide where it will go after you're gone. But what if someone dies and there is no will and no identifiable heir?

If you haven't guessed it, you're probably not going to like the answer. In most cases, the government seizes the unclaimed assets. Each state has its own laws regarding these matters, and most are shaped by the 1954 Uniform Disposition of Unclaimed Property Act. The American Bar Association defines this legislation as a consumer protection law to safeguard property. The more cynical among us define it as a way to fleece the dead.

In fairness, the act can have positive applications. Let's say that for some reason an individual forgets about a bank account or property he or she owned for three to five years. Without the law, these assets would be considered unclaimed, and just about any yahoo could try to swoop in and take them. The state acts as a custodian for the assets and is required to place an advertisement about the seizure in the county paper of the individual's last known address.

It all sounds well intentioned—until you find out the states can use the money they're holding while they're waiting for it to be claimed. Sure, they have to give it back if a legitimate claimant steps forward, but most people have no idea the money is out there.

Furthermore, there are many examples of the government raking in abandoned funds when someone has died without a will and discernable heirs. It's difficult to put a number on the amount of money the government receives in unclaimed assets, but the estimates are high. CNN, for example, has reported that the states collectively sit on nearly fourteen billion dollars in unclaimed assets.

The moral of the story? Make a will. Leave all of your worldly assets to your favorite charity or a good friend. Heck, you can even leave them to the government if you want. Just don't let the government take them. It does enough of that already.

Q What exactly is money laundering?

A You knock over an armored car and suddenly your mattress is overflowing with cash. But if you enjoy your ill-gotten gains by treating yourself to something big—solid-gold yacht, say—the Feds will want to know where the money came from. And if you can't point to a legitimate source, it's off to the big house with you.

When faced with this dilemma, criminals turn to money laundering, the process of making "dirty" money look "clean"—in other words, making it appear that the money is legitimate income. For relatively small amounts of dirty cash, the go-to trick is to set up a front: a business that can record the cash as profit. For example, Al Capone owned Laundromats all over Chicago so that he could disguise the income from his illegal liquor business as laundry profits (how appropriate). There wasn't any way to know how much money people really spent at the Laundromat, so all the profit appeared to be legitimate.

On a larger scale—such as when drug traffickers take in millions—the Laundromat scheme doesn't really work, and things get more complicated. But no matter how elaborate the scheme, you can usually break it down into three basic steps: placement, layering, and integration.

In the placement stage, the goal is to get the hard cash into the financial system, which usually means depositing it into accounts of some kind. In the United States, banks report any transaction greater than ten thousand dollars to the authorities, so one placement strategy is to deposit money gradually, in smaller increments, across multiple bank accounts. Another option is to deposit the money in a bank in a country that has lax financial monitoring laws.

The goal of the next stage—layering—is to shift the money through the financial system in such a complicated way that nobody can follow a paper trail back to the crime. In other words, the criminals are trying to disguise the fact that they are the ones who put the money into the financial system in the first place. Every time launderers move money between accounts, convert it into a different currency, or buy or sell anything—particularly in a country with lax laws—the transaction adds a layer of confusion to the trail.

Finally, in the integration stage, the criminals get the money back by some means that looks legitimate. For example, they might arrange to have an offshore company hire them as generously paid consultants; this way, the money that they earned from their crimes enters their bank accounts as legitimate personal income.

Money laundering is big business, and it's a key foundation for drug trafficking, embezzling, and even terrorism. Many nations have enacted stricter laws and boosted enforcement in order to crack down on money laundering, but they can't put a stop to it unless everyone is vigilant. As long as there are countries with lax financial regulations that trade in the world economy, criminals will have a way to launder their funds.

So, if you've been busily scrubbing your ill-gotten cash in the sink and hanging it on the line to dry, you can stop now. You're doing it wrong.

Q Why are pennies and nickels bigger than dimes?

A It would seem to make sense for the dime (17.91 millimeters in diameter) to be larger than the nickel (21.21 millimeters) and the penny (19.05 millimeters) because it's worth more. But the truth is, the size of a U.S. coin has nothing to do with its value.

When the United States Mint opened in 1792 and produced the first U.S. coins, the metal standard was the silver dollar. All coins were produced in proportionate metallic content to the silver dollar, with the exception of the copper penny. (More on that later.)

The ten-cent coin, or the dime, had one-tenth as much silver as the silver dollar, and the five-cent coin, called the half-dime, had one-twentieth the silver content of the dollar. This meant that the five-cent coin was very small—so small, in fact, that handling it was a challenge. Today's larger five-cent coin, the nickel, is the result of a change in content from silver and copper to copper and nickel back in 1866. Nickel was less expensive than silver—it was cost-effective to manufacture a five-cent piece using this material, and the coin was easier to handle. It also happened to be larger than both the dime and the penny.

The first penny design was actually bigger than today's one-cent piece. It was made of pure copper, and its face bore the image of a woman with flowing hair who symbolized liberty. But in 1857, the shape and size of the penny changed when Congress authorized the U.S. Mint to strike the cent with 88 percent copper and 12 percent nickel, with a shape and size that was determined by the mint director, James Ross Snowden, who chose the dimensions that are still used today.

So even if U.S. coins don't seem to add up, they really do.

Q How are old coins taken out of circulation?

A To answer this question, let's track some money from beginning to end. What follows is the tale of Dimey (a dime) and Bill (a dollar bill).

Dimey is one of the nearly fifteen billion coins that was minted at the United States Mints in Philadelphia and Denver in 2007, and Bill is one of the thirty-eight million notes printed in one day during the same year at the Bureau of Engraving and Printing in Washington, D.C., and Fort Worth, Texas.

Off they go to Federal Reserve Banks around the country, excited to be part of $820 billion in circulation. Their journey isn't finished when they get to the Federal Reserve Banks, though. They still have to go to a couple of commercial banks. There they sit and wait, talking about life, the universe, and the latest episode of *American Idol*—until one day someone withdraws them to pay for a new shirt at a dodgy roadside stall. The owner of the stall then spends Dimey on some candy and uses Bill and some of his dollar friends to get into a baseball game. Thus begins a long, adventure-filled journey for both Dimey and Bill. They meet all sorts of people and grow old and worn.

About twenty-one months later—the normal lifespan for a dollar note—Bill winds up in a bank again. The bank manager takes one look at him and dumps him onto the "unfit" pile. After a while, he is packed up and sent to a Reserve Bank. There, he is cruelly replaced with a younger, hipper dollar bill and is destroyed. (About a third of the money that the Reserve Banks receive is declared unfit and is destroyed.)

Tragic, right? It gets worse.

Meanwhile, Dimey is making the rounds. He meets a cute commemorative-dollar coin down someone's sofa, and they have a brief affair before the dollar is dropped into a jar for safekeeping. Dimey is once again sent on his way. About twenty-five years later, Dimey is old and worn, but he still fits into all the machine slots, so he thinks he's just as good as any of the young whippersnapper dimes.

But one day, he ends up at the same bank where Bill was unceremoniously heaved onto the "unfit" pile years earlier. And the same mean bank manager is still in charge. The manager doesn't like the look of Dimey, either, and sends him to a Reserve Bank. From there, he is put into a box with other worn coins. Next to them is a box that is filled with badly damaged coins.

Off they all go back to the Mint, where they see their shiny new replacements heading off to the banks. Then Dimey and his fellow old coins are tipped into a furnace and melted down.

But it's not all doom and gloom for Dimey and company. In the coin equivalent of reincarnation, they're recycled and become parts of new dimes.

Q Where did the $ sign come from?

A Although the "$" symbol was used in British Colonial America, it was originally associated with Spanish money. The United States didn't have its own coinage until 1793, seventeen years after the Declaration of Independence was adopted. Instead, states printed their own currency; Americans also used money from other countries.

The first U.S. silver dollars were modeled on Spanish dollars, or pesos, which were once known as "pieces of eight." The word "dollar" may not sound Spanish, but back then, it was commonly used in place of "peso." The U.S. coin weighed the same as the Spanish version, so Americans borrowed the name as well: the dollar.

But what about the "$" sign? We searched far and wide for an answer to this pressing question—and we found many. Two popular and credible theories address its origin. One holds that the letters "p" and "s" were used as abbreviations for "peso" by eighteenth-century American writers and accountants. The letters usually appeared as superscript—much as "th" follows numbers, as in "11th." Over time, the loop of the "p" was dropped, so the letter "s" with a line through it came to stand for peso. When the United States adopted the dollar, this symbol was used as well.

The other explanation contends that the dollar sign is derived from the Spanish coat of arms that was stamped onto pesos. Two pillars—the Pillars of Hercules—provided the vertical lines. The "s" was formed by a waving ribbon that joined them.

The Pillars of Hercules were adopted as a symbol of Spain's empire in 1492 by the monarchs Ferdinand and Isabella after Gibraltar came under the kingdom's control. The image appeared on Spanish coins that circulated throughout the New World during the next few centuries.

So that settles things, right? Well, not exactly. There are other explanations, including the notion that the sign comes from the letters "u" and "s." However, the dollar sign was in use before the United States existed. Some people even suggest that the symbol harkens back to the temple of Solomon, or to the Romans or Greeks. But a Spanish origin of the "$" sign makes the most cents...er, sense.

Q Why do we tip some service people but not others?

A The practical reason is that tipping is built into the pay structure for certain jobs. In the United States, employers set wages for certain jobs with the expectation that tips will be a big part of an employee's income. These jobs include restaurant food servers, food-delivery drivers, bartenders, hair stylists, hotel housekeepers, bellhops, taxi drivers, and valets. In many cases, base pay for these jobs is less than minimum wage, and gratuities make up the difference.

You may see tip jars at, say, coffee shops, but Americans don't feel societal pressure to tip on every visit to these establishments. Nor do the livelihoods of the baristas depend on tips. In full-service restaurants, on the other hand, most people know that you should tip a server 15 to 20 percent and that the server depends on this money.

Where did these rules come from? For many "tipping professions," the tradition dates back to the English aristocracy in the seventeenth and eighteenth centuries. When the well-to-do visited each other's estates for extended periods, they typically rewarded the host's servants with "vails"—something extra at the end of stays as thanks for tending to the rooms and other needs. (It would have been simply dreadful not to pay the help. What would it have said about one's own assets?) This type of peer pressure eventually forced vails into common practice at commercial establishments.

The practice took hold among the well-to-do in the United States following the Civil War. Though many people publicly condemned the practice as anti-American because it seemed to propagate the notion of rigidly separated classes, tipping gradually spread beyond homes to the equivalents of domestic servers, maids, valets, and others at inns and restaurants. Americans also began to tip for some additional services (i.e., shoe shining, coat checks, taxis).

Today, tipping traditions are associated with the type of service and not with the wealth of the customer. Eating at the Waffle House may be a far cry from fine dining among the English aristocracy, but Waffle House servers are still part of a tradition that began on seventeenth-century estates. Fast-food workers, on the other hand, don't tend to your needs during a meal, so they fall in the tradition of street vendors, in which tipping never took root. Of course, if you buck the trend and tip them anyway, you might get an extra ketchup packet out of the deal.

Chapter 9
SICKENING STUFF

Q Can you actually get scared to death?

A Scientists say you can. It's not the fear itself that kills you, but the physical reactions that fear provokes. There seem to be two broad types of "death from fear": the kind brought on by a sudden fright and the kind that's provoked by a general sense of dread.

What the heck, let's take the slow version first. A study published in the *British Medical Journal* in 2002 noted that Chinese and Japanese people living in the United States are 13 percent more likely to die on the fourth day of the month than on any other day. This was determined after analyzing 209,908 death certificates of Chinese and Japanese people in America and comparing them with 47,000 Caucasians' death certificates, considering cause of death, inpatient status, age, sex, and marital status for each.

The likely cause of the increase? The dread throughout much of the Asian world of the number four, which is linguistically similar to the word for "death" in Mandarin, Cantonese, and Japanese. It is frightful in the way the number thirteen is in some Western societies—perhaps even more so.

"It is not an all-or-none phenomenon, but the perception of bad luck, a good holiday, or a birthday may shift the odds of dying at that particular time," Stanford psychiatrist David Spiegel, M.D., told *Psychiatric News*, commenting on the study, which was conducted by University of California at San Diego sociologist David P. Phillips, Ph.D. In other words, fear can cause stress that makes the body more vulnerable to death at that time.

This is played out in a more dramatic fashion in sudden death from fear—from fright or shock, to be more accurate. Neurologist Martin A. Samuels, of Brigham and Women's Hospital in Boston, studied hundreds of cases of sudden death and found that catastrophic or intensely frightening events can cause the heart to stop, due to its inability to handle chemicals that the brain sends out during times of great stress.

"We all carry this little bomb inside us," Samuels told ABC News. "It would be like getting an enormous dose of [the drugs] speed or ecstasy." He added, "I know this because I have cases of children with absolutely no heart disease who died on amusement park rides."

And you thought the Fun House was scary.

Q Do people still mummify corpses?

A The ancient Egyptians would be happy to know that five thousand years later, mummification is still around. The processes have changed, but if you want your corpse preserved like King Tut's was, you have options. In fact, you could even end up on the museum circuit, just like the boy king.

Mummification simply means keeping some soft tissue—such as skin or muscle—around long after death. To make a mummy, you just need to keep the tissue from being eaten. Shooing vultures and cannibals away is simple enough, but keeping hungry bacteria at bay is no small feat. The trick is to make the body inhospitable to bacteria. Bacteria like it hot and wet, so mummification depends on keeping a body extremely cold and/or dry.

The ancient Egyptians removed the corpse's internal organs, filled the cavity with linen pads, sprinkled the body with a drying compound called natron, and then wrapped it in bandages. In 1994, Egyptology professor Bob Brier successfully replicated this process—but most other modern mummy-makers use other means.

When Vladimir Lenin croaked in 1924, the Russians decided to mummify him. Their secret process involved immersing the corpse in a chemical bath that replaces all water. The results are impressive—Lenin today looks like Lenin on his deathbed. In 1952, the Argentineans took a similar tack with Eva Peron, the wife of dictator Juan Peron. They replaced bodily fluids with wax, making a wax dummy corpse.

Since 1967, dozens of people have opted for cryonics, a form of mummification in which doctors replace the water in the body with chemicals, and keep the deceased at a crisp -320 degrees Fahrenheit—at least until scientists figure out how to cure death.

The religious organization Summum also offers mummification, but without future reanimation in mind. First, the embalmers immerse the body in a chemical solution for thirty to sixty days to dissolve the water in the body. Next, they wrap the body in gauze and apply a layer of polyurethane, followed by a layer of fiberglass and resin. The body is then sealed in a bronze or stainless steel mummiform capsule. Summun has a growing list of (still-living) human clients. The organization asks for a donation to cover its services, usually $67,000 for the process—not including the mummiform.

The most impressive modern mummies come from a process called Plastination. First, embalmers pump a substance that halts decay into the corpse. Then, they remove the skin and other tissues, and immerse the body in an acetone solution, which dissolves the water and fats. Next, they immerse the body in liquid plastic inside a vacuum chamber and drop the pressure until the acetone boils and evaporates. The resulting vacuum in the body sucks in the plastic so that it permeates every nook and cranny. Before the liquid solidifies into hard plastic, embalmers pose the body. The result is a clean, educational sculpture, which also happens to be an actual corpse.

German anatomist Gunther von Hagens invented Plastination in 1977, and he's signed up nearly eight thousand body donors—many of whom are now mummies in the traveling Body Worlds exhibition. The good news is that it's completely free to join its ranks. To sign up, contact the Institute for Plastination (bodydonation@ plastination.com), review all the gory details, then sign a statement of intent, a stack of consent forms, and a body donor ID card. If you're looking to stick around after you pass on and don't mind posing with tourists for the next few thousand years, the value is hard to beat.

Q Can coffee kill you?

A Sure, if you drink a keg of it. Scientists with too much time on their hands have postulated that you would need to drink between eighty and one hundred cups of coffee—one even says it's more like two hundred cups—in rapid succession before the caffeine somehow fried your system.

Now, it's possible the number is lower than the experts claim. A young woman spent a day in the hospital after drinking seven double espressos at her parents' sandwich shop and experiencing uncontrolled sobbing, serious heart palpitations, breathing problems, and a fever, according to news reports. Could working for your folks really be that painful? Regardless, you'd have to ingest a prodigious—and absurd—amount of coffee before it could kill you.

On the other hand, some coffee each day is good for you in about a million different ways, scientists are now telling us. Curiously, many of the benefits seem greatest in those who are heavy coffee drinkers—and the risks, such as they are, tend to be greater for those who are very light drinkers. For instance, studies have shown a higher risk of heart attack in those who don't regularly drink coffee. For them, even one cup can be harmful, apparently because the caffeine is more of a shock to their system. A researcher said that one cup of coffee for a non-regular coffee drinker could be "the final straw," but one suspects that something else would have felled those subjects anyway, if not a cup of joe.

What are coffee's health benefits? Here's what some studies say:

Coffee might lessen the risk of type 2 diabetes, especially in people who drink more than six cups a day. The risk in such men goes down by more than 50 percent. (However, if you have type 2 diabetes, drinking coffee can put your blood sugar level out of whack.)

Coffee can lower the risk of Parkinson's disease, especially when consumed liberally. Two cups a day can lower the risk of colon cancer by 25 percent and of gallstones by 40 percent or more. Four or more cups a day can lower the risk of cirrhosis of the liver by 80 percent.

Coffee seems to help manage asthma and help control attacks when they happen. It might stop headaches, prevent cavities, and boost athletic performance (more by sharpening the mind than the body). Not a single study has shown that coffee is harmful to kids, and one study suggests that drinking coffee with milk can help kids avoid depression. Nevertheless, the National Institute of Health cautions that caffeine intake by children needs to be carefully monitored.

So, coffee is not for everyone. There are fast and slow caffeine metabolizers—this seems to be genetically determined—and if you're one of the latter, the caffeine hangs out in your body longer and makes you especially susceptible to a kind of nervousness. Coffee blocks certain tension-controlling hormones, so you may be more likely to have a nonfatal heart attack if you drink a couple cups a day. Coffee also has been shown to raise blood pressure slightly and temporarily—but not permanently.

It's common wisdom that every medicine has its benefits and risks, and coffee—though not a controlled substance, thank God—is no different. Despite the occasional scary scientific study (some of which are quickly contradicted) and being a proven risk to those whose tickers are finicky to begin with, coffee seems just a few sips short of a miracle drug. Is that your foot that's tapping nonstop, or mine?

Q Do coffins come with lifetime guarantees?

A How long does a coffin last? Some, like the sarcophagi of the ancient Egyptians, can hold up for centuries. Others, like the Ecopod, a coffin made of recycled newspapers by a British company of the same name, are intended to biodegrade within a few years.

Has any coffin maker offered a lifetime guarantee? Tough question—the best we could find are rumors. People in Indiana have claimed that the state's Batesville Casket Company used to sell caskets with lifetime guarantees, but the company wouldn't confirm this assertion.

Like many casket manufacturers, the Batesville company produces waterproof caskets that are guaranteed not to leak for between twenty and seventy-five years, depending on the price of the casket. Perhaps at one time an overeager funeral director assured grieving families that the deluxe seventy-five-year, leak-proof model would keep their dearly departed safe for at least a lifetime, "guaranteed."

When arranging a funeral, it helps to remember that only the coffin can be guaranteed to last, not the body inside. In fact, the more airtight the coffin, the more rapidly a corpse will disintegrate due to the activity of anaerobic microbes. These bacteria, which thrive in the absence of oxygen, can literally liquefy a dead body. With a little fresh air, a body will decay more slowly. But fast or slow, nature decrees that all bodies inevitably decay, no matter how fancy the coffin.

Q How much booze can you drink without dying?

A A long-suffering fan of the Chicago Cubs must have thought up this question.

Unfortunately, Cubs fans won't find any easy answers here about how much booze they can safely pound during the next soul-crushing defeat. That's because the amount of alcohol that somebody can ingest without dying depends on a huge number of factors. Nevertheless, we can provide some rough guidelines for understanding how alcohol works on the body.

Since we're talking about Cubs fans, let's speak in terms of beer. (For those with broader tastes, experts identify one drink as a twelve-ounce beer, a 1.5-ounce shot, or a five-ounce glass of wine, each of which contains about the same amount of alcohol.) Once imbibed, alcohol enters the bloodstream through the lining of the stomach and small intestine. Most of it is processed and eliminated by the liver (cirrhosis, anyone?)—but the liver can only work so quickly, usually taking care of a little less than one drink's worth per hour. Excess alcohol waits in the bloodstream until the liver can eliminate it.

Drunkenness is gauged by blood alcohol concentration (BAC). BAC measures the percentage of alcohol in the bloodstream at any given time; because heavier people usually have more blood, BAC can be interpreted as a ratio of alcohol-to-body weight. That's why men, who are usually heavier than women, can often drink more than females without appearing drunk. But BAC varies based on many other factors, like the presence of medications in the bloodstream.

Below, we outline the effects of different BAC levels. (A BAC of .01 is one part alcohol to ten thousand parts blood, a BAC of .02 is two parts alcohol to ten thousand parts blood, a BAC of .03 is three parts alcohol to ten thousand parts blood, and so on.)

• .02–.03. A slight elevation of mood; few noticeable effects. As this is generally well before the first pitch, Cubs fans may still be optimistic about the day's game.

• .05–.06. Feelings of relaxation and mild sedation; slightly impaired judgment. This is still well before game time for most Wrigley Field bleacher bums.

• .07–.09. Impaired motor coordination; impaired speech. Cubs fans may have feelings of elation/depression while singing the national anthem.

• .11–.12. Impaired coordination and balance; poor judgment. This is when Cubs fans may accidentally spill their beers into the outfield basket while reaching for a home run that's just been hit by the opposing team.

• .14–.15. Serious problems with motor coordination and judgment; slurred speech; blurred vision. This may be around the third inning, when it seems wise to run onto the field.

• .20. Mental confusion; loss of motor control. Around now, a Cubs fan may start arguing vehemently with the guy next to him that Thad Bosley should be in the Hall of Fame.

• .30. Severe intoxication; hospitalization is necessary. Forget the game—death could result.

• .40–.60. Unconsciousness; coma; possible death. This is not good.

As we said, the number of drinks it would require to reach these levels of BAC varies. But for the typical two-hundred-pound man (this may seem a little heavy, but hey, we're talking about Chicagoans here), one drink in an hour raises his BAC to .02; if the same man were to drink ten Old Styles in that same hour, it would skyrocket to about .19. In order to reach .35 (a level at which some deaths have been reported), he'd have to drink nineteen or twenty Old Styles in an hour.

Because the liver can only work so fast—it can lower the BAC by about .015 per hour, regardless of gender and body weight—the BAC won't decrease at the same rate as it went up. So considering that alcohol sales at Wrigley Field halt after the seventh inning— about two hours into the game—our two-hundred-pound Cubs fan would be able to slam about twenty or twenty-one ridiculously overpriced beers without reaching a lethal BAC level. Then again, our theoretical Cubs fan already knew that.

Q Why was smallpox so deadly for Indians, but not Europeans?

A The Europeans were not good guests in the New World. Whether it was conquistadores in the Caribbean, Pilgrims in New England, sailors in Fiji, or settlers in Australia, they left a calling card no one wanted: diseases that killed thousands of people. Some experts think that smallpox and other diseases, such as measles and influenza, killed up to 95 percent of the native populations of these locales—in other words, only one in twenty people survived.

Yet the Europeans remained ridiculously healthy. And when they sailed back home, they brought no new illnesses with them. Why?

The Europeans had already been exposed to epidemic diseases— or at least their ancestors had. Smallpox was known in ancient Egypt, and a smallpox epidemic killed millions of Romans in the second century AD. The disease hit Europe so frequently that the folks who had no natural immunities died off. Those who lived passed their immunities on to their children. Over the centuries, with so many nasty plagues hitting big population centers, the surviving Europeans became more resistant to the killer microbes.

Where did these diseases originate? Was there a Patient Zero? No. Most of the epidemic bugs—smallpox, measles, influenza, and even tuberculosis—came from livestock. When Asians and Europeans began herding cattle and penning up ducks and pigs thousands of years ago, they breathed in the strange germs that hung around the animals. Once humans started living in cities in large numbers, these germs were able to spread like wildfires. Europe suffered through the same plagues that killed so many Indians and islanders, but

Europe's experience took place hundreds of years earlier, and its populations recovered.

The conquistadores, Pilgrims, sailors, and settlers who crossed the seas during the Age of Exploration came from families that had survived waves and waves of disease. Without realizing it, they brought smallpox, measles, and influenza germs with them to infect people who had never seen cattle, never herded animals, and never, ever been exposed to any of these diseases.

You know the result: Millions died. How many millions is unknown because experts aren't sure about the sizes of pre-encounter populations. The first wave of smallpox to hit Mexico's Aztec Empire in 1520 killed half the kingdom. Up to ten million died, including the emperor. More disease followed, and a century later, the area's native population numbered only 1.6 million.

Here's another infamous example: In 1837, smallpox hit the Mandan, an Indian tribe in North Dakota. The disease, brought by someone who was on a steamboat traveling up the Missouri River, almost destroyed the tribe. Within weeks, the Mandan population of one village dropped from two thousand to forty.

And since no one back then knew about germs, microbes, or how sicknesses spread, the Europeans weren't even aware of what they'd done.

Q Are there still lepers?

A Yes, there are about a quarter-million people worldwide with leprosy. It is found mostly in Southeast Asia and in the Third

World countries of Africa and the Americas, although about a hundred cases are diagnosed in the United States each year. Cures for leprosy were developed in the 1960s and 1970s, and over the past fifty years, the number of afflicted has dropped from more than five million (perhaps as high as twenty million, according to some estimates) to the present figure.

For centuries, lepers were shunned: Healthy men and women wouldn't so much as touch a leper because the grotesque disease was believed to be highly contagious. We now know that it's not—in fact, 95 percent of humans are naturally immune to it. Still, it's easy to see why the disease would have been so frightening. Leprosy starts with a small sore on the skin, which often goes numb as the disease begins to infect the peripheral nerves. If untreated, it can, in extreme cases, cripple and blind its victims.

This rarely happens today. Medicines as common as antibiotics are often effective at fighting leprosy. Patients can be cured of the disease in months or years, which has helped to erase much of its stigma. Doctors now avoid using the term "leprosy" because of its negative connotations and instead call it "Hansen's disease," after Norwegian doctor G. H. Armauer Hansen, who discovered the bacteria that causes it in 1873.

What about all of the awful stories relating to the affliction? Most scientists think that the leprosy described in the Bible was a different sickness than the one that exists today. Hansen's disease does not turn the skin white, for example, so the leprosy of the Old Testament was probably a combination of several other ravaging infections, maybe even cancers.

Leper colonies really existed, from the Middle Ages through the twentieth century. Father Damien's famous leper colony in Hawaii and another colony in Carville, Louisiana, housed most of the Americans who were diagnosed with Hansen's disease before treatments were developed, but there used to be many other centers around the world. Since the disease destroys the nerves and tissues of the body, it would have been horrifying to watch a victim succumb to it. Without a cure or a known cause, doctors thought it best to keep victims segregated from the healthy.

Doctors still aren't entirely sure how Hansen's disease is transmitted, though they suspect that the bacteria pass through the respiratory system. But since the treatments are so effective, and since most folks are immune, the search for an answer doesn't seem as pressing as it once did.

Q Is it still possible to contract Black Death?

A The Black Death is alive and well. But as long as the human population continues to feel that it would rather not willingly share its space with thousands of rats, most people's bodies should remain refreshingly plague-free.

The Black Death killed twenty-five million Europeans from 1347 to 1353, or one-third of the continent's population. The plague is caused by the bacteria *Yersinia pestis*, which mainly spreads when a flea bites an infected rat (or other rodent) for breakfast and then bites a human for lunch or dinner, thus passing on the bacteria. The plague comes in three flavors: bubonic, pneumonic, and septicemic.

Bubonic is the cover girl of the bunch—the one most people associate with the term "plague." The telltale symptom of bubonic plague is buboes, infected lymph nodes on the neck, armpit, and groin. They turn black and ooze blood and puss.

Pneumonic plague occurs when a person inhales the bacteria from someone who is infected. "Cover your mouth when you sneeze," has never made more sense than with this little ditty.

Septicemic plague is when *Yersinia pestis* gets into your bloodstream. It can cause gangrene due to tissue death in extremities like fingers and toes, turning them black. The gangrene and the black buboes and lesions all contributed to the term "Black Death."

Pneumonic and septicemic plague make bubonic plague look like a ray of hope: Untreated, they have close to a 100 percent mortality rate. Bubonic's death rate is a measly 60 to 75 percent if left untreated.

The fact that most people live in much more sanitary conditions these days means that the chances of getting the plague are low. However, it is still very much around. In India, between August and October 1994, 693 people contracted the plague, and fifty-six of them died. Ten to fifteen cases are reported every year in the United States, and there are one thousand to three thousand annual cases globally. Animals that carry the plague are found in Asia, Africa, and North and South America. Additionally, plague is a perfect candidate for biological warfare, particularly pneumonic plague since it can be airborne.

Treatment includes a very aggressive dose of antibiotics, which must begin early to improve the chance of survival. The Centers for Disease Control and Prevention recommends that people traveling in rural places that might harbor the disease take precautions against it. Those with the highest risk should start on preemptive antibiotics. Others should use insect repellent on their bodies and clothing.

So, if you're traveling in an area where you could be bitten by a plague-carrying flea, try to stick to bed-and-breakfasts run by human beings and skip the rodent-owned ones. Nothing ruins a vacation like the Black Death.

Q What is the worst way to die?

A The psychologist Ernest Becker posited that we're so preoccupied with cheating death that we don't actually live, in a meaningful sense anyway. His suggestion is that the worst type of death is one that follows an insignificant life. This sounds like a load of bull to us, and we'd rather live an insignificant life with a relatively painless death than, say, be consumed in a fire or devoured by hungry piranhas.

Speaking of wasting large amounts of time thinking about death, some people do it as a career—they're known as thanatologists. Some journalists also have spent a lot of effort on the subject, including Anna Gosline, who wrote a long article for *The New Scientist* in 2007 in which she established two things: First, there are a lot of nasty ways to die; and second, she is a most curious person who would not be our first choice to take out to dinner, but who might be fun on Halloween.

Gosline's summary of a range of common painful deaths is

magisterial. Here's a sampling of her findings:

• Bleeding to death. This was the Roman aristocracy's favorite form of suicide. The Romans would crawl into a warm tub, nick a vein, and slowly be carried off to the afterlife, full of self-righteous satisfaction at having thumbed their noses at the disagreeable emperors who were infringing on their wealthy prerogatives. Weakness, thirst, anxiety, dizziness, and confusion are common stages before unconsciousness from blood loss—but then, that sounds like a normal day for many of us.

• Burning to death. As in frat houses and newsrooms, it's the toxic gases that get most victims. But those who die directly from a fire's flames suffer immensely, as the inflammatory response to burns only increases the pain.

• Decapitation. Unless it's a botched job—as with Margaret Pole, the Countess of Salisbury, who fought her executioner in 1541 and was hit eleven times with the axe before succumbing—this seems relatively painless. Full-on death occurs in no more than seven seconds, when the brain's oxygen is used up. Of course, that means you would live for a few seconds after the blow, though that's only scientific speculation. Headless focus-group subjects are hard to rustle up.

• Falling. Like drowning, this no doubt frightens many people the most, because it can happen in the course of everyday life. Survivors have reported the sensation of time slowing down, and feeling alert and focused on maintaining an upright position and landing feet-first—an instinct we share with cats and other animals.

• Hanging. Apart from the awful dread that can only build from the moment you realize the jig is up, this is relatively quick and painless—unless the hangman's a hack and your fall is too short or the noose is poorly tied, in which case the struggle at the end of the rope is mighty uncomfortable.

Okay, we've had just about enough of this disconcerting topic, and we didn't even touch on crucifixion, lethal injection, the electric chair, and many other forms of death, natural and unnatural. Our personal un-favorite is an airplane crash, but frankly, we're too darned terrified of such a scenario to discuss it. Maybe Anna Gosline is free.

Q Which is the world's healthiest country?

A Have you swallowed a mouthful of seaweed and raw fish recently? If so—and if it wasn't related to some sort of harrowing near-death experience at the beach—you just might live in *Foreign Policy* magazine's choice for the world's healthiest country: Japan.

Foreign Policy lauded the Land of the Rising Sun for its low rates of heart disease and cancer (thanks in part to its population's rice consumption and "ocean fresh" diet), as well as its widespread cultural emphasis on physical fitness. These qualities have helped to produce an average life expectancy of seventy-nine years for men and an amazing eighty-six years for women.

Japan also finished first on a list of healthy countries that was compiled by the World Health Organization (WHO). The WHO uses a unique system to estimate the number of years the average person in a given country will live his or her life in "full health." The Japanese topped the charts at 74.5 years. Next, in order: Australia, France, Sweden, and Spain. The United States finished a dismal twenty-fourth. Dr. Christopher Murray, director of the WHO's global program on evidence for health policy, offered this cheery pronouncement: "Basically you die earlier and spend more time disabled if you're an American rather than a member of most other advanced countries."

It's not all gloom and doom for the Krispy Kreme Nation, however. *Forbes* magazine compiled a similar list and pegged the United States at number eleven, while Japan didn't even crack the top fifteen. (Iceland was first.) *Forbes* used a formula that took into account a broad array of factors, including air pollution, access to good drinking water and sanitation, and the number of doctors per capita.

Uncle Sam fared even better in a survey that was published by *Men's Health* magazine, which ranked the U.S. as the world's fifth-healthiest place to live—if you're a man. Of particular note to the authors of this study was our ability to restrain the smoking habit; only 19 percent of American men smoke, and 70 percent of U.S. workers are protected by no-smoking regulations. Japan didn't appear on the *Men's Health* list of healthiest countries, but it's worth remembering that this publication devotes as much scientific analysis to compiling "The World's Hottest Places to Have Sex" as it does to determining the world's healthiest nations.

By the way, Japan didn't make *Men's Health*'s "Hottest Places to Have Sex" list, either. Apparently, seaweed isn't much of an aphrodisiac.

Q Which profession has the highest suicide rate?

A Writers. Just kidding. We frequently hear that dentists have the highest suicide rate, but this is nothing more than an urban legend, perhaps fueled by the reputation that dentists have as dour people who inflict a distinctly unpleasant kind of pain. The American Dental Association itself researched the claim and discovered it to be false.

For many years, there wasn't a clear answer to this question, due to a lot of factors. For one thing, death certificates, which many studies used to provide data, are notoriously inaccurate; suicides are sometimes registered as "accidents" to protect the deceased's family and reputation. And some have argued that trying to correlate suicide and profession is iffy because it doesn't answer the obvious cause-and-effect questions that arise, such as: Which came first, the profession or the impulse to commit suicide?

Regardless, a study of data from twenty-four states from 1984 to 1988 concluded that "food batchmakers"—food processors who operate mixers, blenders, and other cooking machines—were the most suicide-prone, by a wide margin (almost 10 percent) over the next-highest group, physicians and health aides (excluding nurses). Lathe operators came next, at a rate that was almost 10 percent lower than that of physicians.

This study didn't convince everyone, but a more recent one might. A 2003 article in a major medical journal concentrated on doctors, calling medicine the most suicide-prone of all professions and suggesting that untreated depression is the culprit. While the study showed that male doctors have the same rate of depression as the male population in general, their rate of suicide is about 40 percent higher. In female doctors, depression is likewise at the same rate as the general female population, but suicide is more than twice as frequent.

The study authors suggested that doctors feel pressure to not admit or treat their depression, perhaps because they feel a need to uphold reputations and maintain their own personal senses of being as healers and not patients. They also have access to lethal drugs and, based on their high "suicide-completion" rate, it appears they know how to use them.

Heard enough? We have. But what this suggests is that the next time your physician asks you how you feel, you should do the good doctor a favor by asking, "How do *you* feel? Want to talk about it?"

Q Why do they sterilize the needle before lethal injection?

A The United States is a nation terrified of germs. Inundated by media reports of flu pandemics, new strains of drug-resistant tuberculosis, untreatable "superbugs," and mysterious flesh-eating bacteria, Americans put paper on toilet seats, push disinfected carts at the grocery store, and buy millions of dollars worth of antibacterial hand gel each year. Americans also, for some reason, sterilize needles before lethally injecting condemned prisoners. Seems a little overboard, doesn't it?

Actually, there are many reasons for the use of sterilized needles in lethal injections, the most obvious being to protect the lethal injector. A slip of the hand, an inadvertent twitch, a poorly timed sneeze— one can imagine a number of scenarios in which the needle might go astray.

Indeed, the history of capital punishment in the United States is littered with bungled executions that would be amusing if they weren't so disturbing. Poison gas has been improperly administered, needles have shot from veins mid-injection, and in more than one case, the heads of electrocuted inmates have burst into flames. By far the largest number of botched executions has come via lethal injection, though usually the biggest problem is finding a suitable vein to insert the needle (as a number of death-row inmates are habitual drug users).

A second reason for sterilization is the rare possibility (though perhaps less rare now, in the age of DNA evidence) that the criminal could be exonerated or earn a stay of execution at the very last moment—perhaps even after the needle has been inserted. We can hear you now: "Oh, come on! That would never happen!" *Au contraire.* Consider the case of James Autry, convicted of the April 1980 murder of two people at a convenience store in Texas. In October 1983, Autry's turn on the lethal injection gurney (doesn't quite have the same grim ring as the electric chair, does it?) finally came. He was strapped down, the IV inserted into his vein. Onlookers leaned forward in anticipation. Suddenly, just as the sodium thiopental was about to be administered, the proceedings were interrupted with word that Autry had been granted a stay of execution by a Supreme Court judge, and Autry was unhooked.

Sounds like the stuff of Hollywood, doesn't it? Not really. In March 1984, Autry was executed anyway. It was Texas, after all.

Chapter 10
ODD ORIGINS OF THINGS

Q Why do the Chinese represent each year with an animal?

A To Westerners, 2009 was the twelve months between December 2008 and January 2010. But to the Chinese, it was the Year of the Ox. Chinese New Year traditionally falls in late January or early February and kicks off a period that's named for a particular animal. If you're not familiar with the Chinese zodiac—or haven't been to a Chinese restaurant where it's colorfully displayed on placemats—you may be wondering how this curious tradition got started.

The Chinese zodiac is based on the lunisolar calendar, which is governed by the solar year and the phases of the moon. It assigns an animal to hours within a day, periods within a year, and individual years. The Chinese zodiac rotates on a twelve-year cycle and the animals, in order, are: rat, ox, tiger, rabbit or hare, dragon, snake, horse, sheep or ram, monkey, rooster, dog, and pig. Each animal has specific traits that are said to determine a person's personality as well as foretell events.

And while the Chinese zodiac's exact origin is unknown, there are many theories about why these particular animals were chosen. One holds that they're related to an ancient system of telling time known as the Ten Celestial Stems and the Twelve Earthly Branches. It was used in China as early as the Shang Dynasty, possibly around 1122 BC. Familiar animals were chosen to represent each of the Twelve Earthly Branches because the average person of the day could not read or perform the calculations that were necessary to determine the time.

In this system, the animals are ordered based on their number of hooves or toes, and they alternate between odd and even numbers. For example, a rat has five toes on its back feet, so it is the first animal. The second animal, the ox, has four hooves. This made the order of the animals easy to remember, although it doesn't quite explain why these particular animals were chosen in the first place.

According to another theory, the animals and their places in the order are explained by the correlation between the natural activities of the beasts and certain times of the day or night. The Ten Celestial Stems and the Twelve Earthly Branches divide a twenty-four-hour day into twelve two-hour periods. To tell the time, you'd have to know, for example, that rats are supposedly most active between 11:00 P.M. and 1:00 A.M., that snakes (the sixth animal) begin to come out of their dens between 9:00 A.M. and 11:00 A.M., and that pigs aren't sleeping soundly until between 9:00 P.M. and 11:00 P.M.

The most fanciful explanation suggests that the Chinese zodiac originated in a race that was set up by the Jade Emperor, a legendary mythic and religious figure in Taoism. He invited every animal in existence to participate in the race, but only twelve showed up. The rat won, which is why it is first in the zodiac. The other animals are ordered according to how they finished in the race. The lumbering pig came in last.

Regardless of it origins, some people believe in the Chinese zodiac every bit as fiercely as others believe in the Western zodiac. And others say with a smirk that whether you think of yourself as a Snake or a Taurus, the whole thing should be taken with a grain of salt.

Q Why is Thanksgiving on Thursday?

A Because Abraham Lincoln said so. In his 1863 proclamation, Lincoln declared Thanksgiving to be an official national holiday. It was one way he attempted to unite the nation in the midst of the brutal Civil War. Here's what he said:

"I do therefore invite my fellow citizens in every part of the United States, and also those who are at sea and those who are sojourning in foreign lands, to set apart and observe the last Thursday of November next, as a day of Thanksgiving and Praise to our beneficent Father who dwelleth in the Heavens."

Thanksgiving was celebrated long before Honest Abe came along and gave a speech about it. According to American tradition, the Pilgrims' first Thanksgiving was observed in 1621 (it probably took place in mid-October, and no one knows for sure on which day of the week). Although the Pilgrims did not celebrate Thanksgiving the following year, over time it became a tradition for days of thanksgiving to be celebrated throughout the colonies following the fall harvest. But not all the colonies honored Thanksgiving, and not all observed is on the same day.

A unified Thanksgiving Day came about largely due to the efforts of Sarah Josepha Hale. As editor of the popular magazine *Godey's Lady Book,* Hale campaigned for a single, national day of thanksgiving for a number of years—until Lincoln granted his support in 1863. That year, Thanksgiving was celebrated on Thursday, November 26.

Why Thursday? Well, it was good enough for George Washington, who declared a one-time national day of thanksgiving on a Thursday in late November 1789. In addition, according to *The Old Farmer's Almanac,* Thursday might have become a traditional day of thanksgiving for the Puritans in order to distance the commemoration from the Sabbath day.

In 1939, President Franklin Roosevelt announced that Thanksgiving would be celebrated on the third Thursday of November instead of the last. This was an attempt to encourage earlier holiday shopping and boost the economy during the Great Depression. But not all the states complied until Congress passed a resolution in 1941 declaring that Thanksgiving would fall on the fourth Thursday of November, and that's where it remains today. Kind of makes you crave a piece of pumpkin pie, huh?

Q Why do chefs wear those ridiculous hats?

A As anybody who has ever worked in a restaurant can attest, the chef is the supreme dictator of the kitchen. Sometimes brilliant, often tempestuous, the chef rules the back of the house through a combination of respect and fear. Still, how can someone wearing such a ridiculous hat be taken seriously?

Outside of the pope, chefs may have the silliest headgear in the professional world. It's called a *toque blanche*, and it is a white, heavily starched embarrassment whose look ranges from a tall tube to an enormous, deformed mushroom.

Just how it came to be the symbol of chefdom is a matter of debate. Indeed, there are several theories about the origin of the chef's toque, none of which is substantiated with enough evidence to be confirmed as a sole explanation. One of these is that Henry VIII, outraged at finding a hair in his soup, ordered the beheading of his chef. Future chefs took note, making sure to cover their heads in order to save them.

A second theory holds that the chef's toque originated in ancient Assyria, long before the birth of Christ. Back then, poisoning was the favored method of assassination (hence, the dangerous profession of the royal food taster). Obviously, a chef was under scrutiny because he had the power to poison food. Proof of the chef's allegiance to his royal master was a "crown" he fashioned—a tall hat, made of cloth, that mimicked the actual crown worn by the king himself.

A third theory, and perhaps the most compelling, is that the toque originated in the sixth century AD, in the beginning of the Middle Ages. In those dark days, artists and intellectuals—groups that included chefs—were persecuted, and it was said that some of these luminaries protected themselves by taking shelter in monasteries. To disguise themselves, they donned the wardrobe of the clergy, which apparently included silly hats.

Though the earliest origins of the toque are debatable, it is known that the headwear evolved into its current form in France, the birthplace of *haute cuisine*. By the nineteenth century, forms of the toque were worn all over Europe, though their shapes varied.

In the late nineteenth century, the legendary French chef Auguste Escoffier brought order to the chaos and came up with a standard toque. Unfortunately, he decided that the tall, starched version of the chef's hat was ideal. In a way, it's not entirely surprising that the toque would find its ultimate form in France. It is the country, after all, that gave us another of the all-time silliest hats: the beret.

Q What's the story behind the Tooth Fairy?

A Tracking down the Tooth Fairy is tricky business. There are a myriad of fictional accounts, all of which gnaw away at the pixie's true origin. The Tooth Fairy's tale has been told in everything from children's books featuring dainty sprites to films portraying calcium junkies who try to eat through your bones.

What is the real story behind the gal who takes teeth that are placed beneath pillows and pays for the privilege? The Tooth Fairy has been popular in the United States for a century and has its—ahem—roots in many cultures. According to one theory, the Tooth Fairy as we know her today was influenced mainly by a French fairy tale from the eighteenth century titled *La Bonne Petite Souris*. The tale features a mouse that is transformed into a fairy and helps a good queen defeat an evil king by sneaking under his pillow and knocking out his teeth.

Perhaps with some inspiration from this good-hearted little tooth-mouse, the American Tooth Fairy appeared early in the twentieth century as a benevolent female spirit who specialized in giving gifts, like Santa Claus and the Easter Bunny. The first-known story of the Americanized Tooth Fairy is the 1927 play *The Tooth Fairy*, by Esther Watkins Arnold. The first children's book centered on the sprite—*The Tooth Fairy*, by Lee Rogow—was published in 1949.

Since then, the Tooth Fairy has carved out a spot in the heart of American culture. There was even a museum in Deerfield, Illinois, dedicated to the Tooth Fairy. Founded by the late Dr. Rosemary Wells—formerly of Northwestern University's department of dentistry—and run out of her home, the museum held an eye-popping, teeth-grinding amount of Tooth Fairy memorabilia.

It's easy to see how Wells was able to acquire so much stuff. American capitalism has spawned Tooth Fairy pillows, purses, books, and even horror movies—the Tooth Fairy is big business. This glut of goods led us to concoct our own jaded theory about the origin of the Tooth Fairy, which goes like this:

In 1935, the United States government started a top-secret project called "The Tooth Fairy Program." Curiously, this was around the same time the Social Security Act was introduced. The government needed a way to protect its citizens in case Social Security failed, so special agents, dubbed "fairies," were tasked with sneaking into children's rooms to trade cash for teeth. The program was meant to introduce the youth of America to the idea of saving money.

As happens all too often, some of the agents were corrupt and skimmed money off the top. After World War II, the government yanked the program as a dentist would an impacted molar. Parents, however, kept the tradition alive, and that's how we ended up where we are today. Seems about as plausible as the origin offered in *La Bonne Petite Souris*, right?

Q Why do we carve jack-o'-lanterns?

A Who doesn't fondly remember the Halloweens of yore? You'd choose a big orange pumpkin from a local farm, cut off the top to scoop out the mushy insides, and spend an entire evening painstakingly carving out the features. Then finally, with tired eyes, aching fingers, and a sense of pride, you'd place your glowing work of art on the front porch...where it would last about 18.4 minutes before some kid would smash it into smithereens.

Though the practice seems somewhat futile in our pumpkin-smashing present, the tradition of carving jack-o'-lanterns dates back centuries. There is no definitive explanation for how present-day jack-o'-lanterns came into being, but we do know that ancient Celts—as well as other sects of the era—believed that flames would ward off evil spirits.

In the Celtic tradition, the harvest season ended on November 1. This date, according to Celtic legend, also signified a dangerous event: a time when the boundary between the living and dead blurred. For one day, potentially harmful spirits could wreak havoc on the living. To keep these spirits at bay, ancient people built large bonfires as part of their end-of-harvest festivals—festivals that live on today as Halloween celebrations.

But why do we carve jack-o'-lanterns? In the absence of documented evidence, most people cite an Irish folktale called "Stingy Jack."

In a small Irish village, the legend goes, lived a deceitful, lying, drunken fellow named Jack. He was also a cheap bastard, so he was known to the locals as Stingy Jack. One evening, Stingy Jack, out on a drunken spree, ran into the devil, who informed Jack that due to his derelict behavior, he was going to hell. The devil asked Jack to kindly prepare his soul to be taken. Jack suggested a drink beforehand. The devil—apparently a truly Irish evil spirit—agreed.

When the bill came, the devil and Stingy Jack looked at each other awkwardly. Stingy Jack reminded the devil of his nickname and said that he had a reputation to uphold. The devil informed Jack that Lucifer, Lord of Hell, didn't buy people drinks. The barkeeper said he didn't care who they were—no one drank for free.

They were at a stalemate, but then Jack had an idea: What if the devil transformed himself into a silver coin with which Jack would pay their bill? The devil, who had perhaps had a few too many drinks, inexplicably thought this to be a brilliant idea. Upon transformation, though, Jack promptly put the numismatic devil into his pocket, along with a silver crucifix to prevent the devil from reverting to form. It was only after he extracted a promise from the devil to not take his soul that Jack released the captive demon.

Much later, when Stingy Jack died, he was denied entrance to heaven. The devil also refused him entrance at the gates of hell, citing the promise he had made long before. He did, however, offer Jack a perpetually glowing piece of coal. Stingy Jack was doomed to wander the countryside for eternity, with nothing but his glowing coal from hell to light the way.

To ward off the spirit of Stingy Jack—also known as "Jack of the Lantern"—people in ancient Ireland, Scotland, and England began to carve scary faces into hollowed-out turnips and potatoes. When the first British settlers came to North America, legend suggests that they continued the tradition, using the native North American pumpkin. It was, after all, larger, simpler to carve, and easier to smash into smithereens.

Q Do the kings and queens on playing cards depict anyone real?

A The beer is cold, the cigars are burning, and the wives are watching *Grey's Anatomy*. This can mean only one thing: poker night for the boys. And on this occasion, you're about to win a huge pile of chips because all the cards in your hand have faces on them. You lay the cards down, do a little bragging, and the fun goes on. But have you ever wondered whose faces are on those cards?

Some playing card enthusiasts swear that the kings and queens represent real figures from history. This isn't the case with today's playing cards—unless you get one of those decks that has the fifty-two greatest Notre Dame football players or fifty-two poses of Elvis Presley (skinny Elvis is always king). At one time, however, the pictures on playing cards did indeed depict real people.

Playing cards probably made their way to Europe from the Middle East during the fourteenth century. The Spaniards and the Italians were among the first Europeans to make playing cards, in the second half of the fourteenth century. But the French, who became the main producers of playing cards, jump-started the trend of using illustrations of real people.

In the fifteenth century, French card masters started creating pictorial identities for all the court cards. The card masters decided who would appear on the cards based, it appears, on nothing more than personal preference. Consider it the first political opinion poll. Apparently, some of the first kings to be represented on cards were Solomon, a king of Israel; Clovis, a king of the Franks; and Constantine, a Roman emperor.

During the lifetime of France's Henry IV (1553–1610), the cards were somewhat standardized. The kings most often represented were Charlemagne, a king of the Franks (hearts); David, a king of Israel (spades); Julius Caesar, a Roman emperor (diamonds); and Alexander, a king of Macedon (clubs).

The queens have been the objects of conjecture because the illustrations aren't as identifiable, although each had a name: The queen of hearts was Judith, who may have represented the Empress Judith of Bavaria; the queen of diamonds was Rachel, who may have represented the Biblical Rachel; the queen of spades was Pallas, who may have represented Joan of Arc or the Greek goddess Pallas Athena; and the queen of clubs was Argine, who may have represented the wife of Charles VII, king of France. There are other possibilities, too, ranging from Juno, the Roman queen of the Gods, to Agnes Sorel, the mistress of Charles VII.

Mistresses on playing cards? Think of the intrigue that would add to a poker night on Capitol Hill.

Q How many human languages are there?

A *Moi! Natya! Malo! O-si-yo!* That's hello in Finnish, Kikuyu, Samoan, and Cherokee, respectively. How many different languages are there? By one count: 6,912. That's a lot of hellos. It's also a lot of good-byes: Nearly five hundred of these languages have fewer than one hundred fluent speakers and are in danger of dying out within a generation.

By contrast, Mandarin Chinese is spoken by about 1.05 billion people. This includes both the 882 million native speakers and 178 million who speak it as a second language, adding up to nearly a sixth of the world's population. Hindi/Urdu or Hindustani, the primary language of the subcontinent of India, is spoken natively by 451 million people and by another 453 million as a second language. English comes in third with 337 million native speakers, plus 350 million who use it as a second language.

At the bottom of the list are Comanche, a Native American language with only two hundred fluent speakers; Livonian, a Latvian language spoken by thirty-five people; and a combination of Sami dialects from the reindeer herding tribes of northern Scandinavia with fewer than forty speakers each.

Who's counting languages, and why? For many years, the *Ethnologue* has been the most reliable source of information on world languages. This organization, started by Christian missionaries who were interested in translating the Bible into every known language, partnered with the International Organization for Standardization in 2002 to create a coding system for tracking languages. Recently, the *Observatoire de Linguistique*, a European research network, and *Encarta,* the encyclopedia published by Microsoft, have also released their own language indices.

Not all of these sources agree. There may be as few as five thousand languages or as many as eleven thousand, depending on which method linguists use to distinguish dialects from full-fledged languages. They all reach the same conclusion, however: As the globe's population increases, the number of unique languages decreases. Every language, no matter how obscure, represents part of humanity's cultural inheritance. Some researchers have concluded that half the world's current languages will die out by the end of the twenty-first century, taking much of their history, music, and literature with them.

Fortunately, the future of linguistic diversity may not be that dire. Languages can demonstrate surprising resiliency. Witness the persistence of Yiddish. Not so dead yet, *nu?* However, Walmajarri (Australia, one thousand speakers), Inuinnaqtun (Canada, two thousand speakers), and Culina (Peru/Brazil, 1,300 speakers) may not be so lucky.

Maybe we should all brush up on our language skills before it's too late. Get a bilingual dictionary, take a deep breath, and learn how to say, "Hello."

Q Is it true that Eskimos have a thousand words for snow?

A It stands to reason that the Eskimos would have a lot of words for snow. Their lives revolve around the stuff, after all. But it seems that reports of the exact number of words have, well, snowballed.

There are five major Eskimo languages. The most widely used is Inuit, which is spoken by people living in northern Alaska, Canada, and Greenland. The notion that Eskimos have lots of words for snow started with anthropologist Frank Boas, who spent much of the late nineteenth century living with Eskimos in British Columbia and on Baffin Island of Upper Canada.

He wrote in the introduction to his 1911 *Handbook of North American Indians* that the Inuit language alone had four words for snow: *aput* ("snow on the ground"), *qana* ("falling snow"), *piqsirpoq* ("drifting snow"), and *qimuqsoq* ("a snowdrift").

Boas believed that differences in cultures were reflected in differences in language structure and usage. This wasn't to say that Inuits saw snow differently, according to Boas, but that they organized their thinking and their vocabulary about snow in a more complex manner because snow was such a big part of their daily lives.

In 1940, anthropologist Benjamin Whorf claimed that the Eskimo/Inuit language contained seven words for snow. In 1984, Steven Jacobson published the *Yup'ik Eskimo Dictionary*, which placed the figure for the Yup'ik Eskimos at well into the hundreds. Exaggeration piles upon exaggeration, and pretty soon a thousand words for snow sounds quite reasonable.

In a July 1991 article critiquing Jacobson's dictionary, University of Texas linguist Anthony Woodbury claimed the problem is lexemes. Lexemes are individual units of meaning: For example, the word "speak" can be transformed into the words spoken, speech, speaking, spoke, and so on. Woodbury noted that noun lexemes in at least one of the Eskimo languages can be arranged into more

than 250 different individual words or phrases, and verbs allow
for even more differentiations. He claimed that there were only
fifteen individual lexemes for snow shared among the five Eskimo
languages. That's not all that different from the English language.

Q Is sign language the same in all languages?

A Nope. There are many different sign languages in use around
the world. French-speaking nations have their own sign
language, as do Spanish-speaking countries. But that doesn't mean
sign language is a sort of gestural translation of the local vernacular.
Two countries that share a spoken language—like the United
States and England—can end up using completely different signing
systems. In fact, American Sign Language actually has more in
common with its French counterpart than with British Sign Language.
To understand why this is, you have to look at where modern sign
languages were developed: in the early schools for the deaf.

The first of these institutions was opened in France in the mid-
eighteenth century by Charles-Michel, abbé de l'Epée. Other
educators before him had tutored deaf children from well-to-
do families, but Charles-Michel sought to help the poorest deaf
children, who otherwise would have been pushed to the fringes
of society. In his school, he developed a rudimentary system for
signing letters and whole words.

In the early nineteenth century, Thomas Gallaudet of Hartford,
Connecticut, wanted to establish a school for the deaf in the United
States. He raised money and traveled across the Atlantic to observe
European teaching methods so that he could emulate them in his
own school. The English refused to share their techniques with him,

but the French welcomed him. He returned to Connecticut, bringing with him the sign language developed by Charles-Michel, and in 1817, he established the school that is now known as the American School for the Deaf.

The French method of signing that Charles-Michel taught his students gradually spread to schools around the United States. Combined with other local signing systems, it became American Sign Language (ASL), which is a living language—one to which new signs are added—and is among the most complete sign languages in the world.

Linguists estimate that more than half of the signs in French Sign Language and ASL overlap, due to their common origins. It's likely that a deaf person from France and one from the United States could communicate easily. British Sign Language, on the other hand, has little in common with ASL, so there is a much more profound communication barrier between deaf people from different parts of the English-speaking world.

International Sign Language, formerly known as Gestuno, is used for conferences such as the World Federation of the Deaf and the Deaflympics, but it's a separate language with a unique system of signs. The bottom line? Just like those that are spoken, sign languages are rich, diverse, and expressive.

Q Why is America called America?

A Weren't you paying attention in your eighth-grade world history class? As you were undoubtedly told, the Americas are named for the Italian explorer Amerigo Vespucci. But what did he do that was so great? The only fact about his life that anyone seems to remember is that, well, America is named after him. How did a dude who's otherwise forgotten by history manage to stamp his name on two entire continents?

While he didn't make the lasting impression of his contemporary Christopher Columbus, Vespucci was no slouch. As a young man, he went to work for the Medici family of Florence, Italy. The Medicis were powerbrokers who wielded great influence in politics (they ran the city), religion (some were elected to be bishops and popes), and art (they were the most prominent patrons of the Renaissance, commissioning some of the era's most memorable paintings, frescos, and statues).

Like many of the movers and shakers of that age, the Medici had an interest in exploration, which is where Vespucci came in. Under their patronage, he began fitting out ships in Seville, where he worked on the fleet for Columbus's second voyage. Vespucci evidently caught the exploration bug while hanging around the port—between 1497 and 1504 he made as many as four voyages to the South America coast, serving as a navigator for Spain and later Portugal. On a trek he made for Portugal in 1501, Vespucci realized that he wasn't visiting Asia, as Columbus believed, but a brand-spankin' new continent. This "ah-ha" moment was his chief accomplishment, though he also made an extremely close calculation of Earth's circumference (he was only fifty miles off).

Vespucci's skills as a storyteller are what really put his name on the map. During his explorer days, Vespucci sent a series of letters about his adventures to the Medici family and others. Vespucci livened up ho-hum navigational details with salacious accounts of native life, including bodice-ripping tales of the natives' sexual escapades. Needless to say, the dirty letters were published and proved to be exceedingly popular. These accounts introduced the term "The New World" to the popular lexicon.

German cartographer Martin Waldseemüller was a fan, so he decided to label the new land "America" on a 1507 map. He explained his decision thusly: "I do not see what right any one would have to object to calling this part after Americus, who discovered it and who is a man of intelligence, [and so to name it] *Amerige*, that is, the Land of Americus, or *America*: since both Europa and Asia got their names from women."

But there are those who believe that Vespucci's forename wasn't the true origin of the name. Some historians contend that the term "America" was already in use at the time and that Waldseemüller incorrectly assumed it referred to Vespucci. Some have suggested that European explorers picked up the name *Amerrique*—"Land of the Wind" in Mayan—from South American natives. Others say it came from a British customs officer named Richard Ameryk, who sponsored John Cabot's voyage to Newfoundland in 1497 and possibly some pre-Columbian explorations of the continent. Yet another theory claims that early Norse explorers called the mysterious new land *Ommerike*, meaning "farthest outland."

In any case, the name ended up on Waldseemüller's map in honor of Vespucci. The map proved to be highly influential; other cartographers began to use "America," and before long it had stuck. Keep this story in mind the next time you're composing a heart-stoppingly boring email—if you sex it up a bit, you might get a third of the world named after you.

Q Why are fire engines red?

A Give a youngster a box of crayons, ask for a drawing of a fire engine, and watch those little fingers reach for red. Kids know that red is the right color for a fire truck—it's adults who don't always agree.

Precisely why fire engines are red is lost in the smoky recesses of history. Experts from such agencies as the U.S. Fire Administration and the National Fire Protection Association (NFPA) cite theories, but even they admit that no one knows for sure. Most conjecture leads to the nineteenth century, when firefighting in America was an ad hoc pursuit and competition between public, private, and volunteer brigades was fierce. Crews would race each other to a blaze, and the first group on the scene took control. Sometimes it was to secure a claim on any fire-insurance money; often it was just for the glory. The rivalry extended to uniforms and equipment: The brighter and more elaborate, the more prestigious. Not only was red the shade most identified with fire, it was the most regal and expensive color with which to paint the firefighting apparatus. Thus was born a tradition.

Another theory holds that red became the accepted color for safety reasons in the early twentieth century, when most automobiles were black and red was thought to stand out best in traffic. Indeed, the visibility of fire trucks to other motorists remains a matter of grave importance. NFPA records show a steady increase in the number of collisions involving fire-emergency vehicles going to or from a blaze. In 2006, for instance, there were 16,020 such collisions, resulting in 1,250 injuries and the deaths of nineteen firefighters.

Safety concerns once led to a flirtation with alternatives to fire-engine red. The movement was fueled by research suggesting that hues of yellow or lime are more visible to the human eye, particularly at dusk or nighttime since they are more reflective. Indeed, support for a switch to yellow, lime green, or white from red was strong in the 1970s and 1980s. But subsequent analysis revealed little difference in the number of collisions.

It turns out that color has virtually no effect on how visible a fire truck is to motorists, but lighting and reflective surfaces do. The NFPA never had a requirement for fire truck color, but in 1991 it established new standards that increased the number and size of emergency lights and specified their brightness and location. It also added standards for the size, placement, and color of reflective striping. Though the Federal Aviation Administration stuck with lime-yellow for airport emergency vehicles, municipal fire departments have trended back to red. (Contrasting black or white upper bodies are considered chic for the best-dressed trucks.) The government's Occupational Safety and Health Administration also favors red in its standards.

Most firefighters couldn't be happier. They say that the public never really associated lime with fire trucks, and anything other than red somehow bucked a proud tradition. Any kid with a crayon in his hand could have told you as much.

Q Why do people wear costumes on Halloween?

A Why do we deck ourselves out like Spider-Man or the Wicked Witch of the West on Halloween? When you think about it, it's a pretty silly way to celebrate the eve of All Saints' Day. Turns out that dressing in masks and costumes started along with trick-or-treating about three hundred and fifty years ago.

The earliest mention of wearing disguises on Halloween comes from Ireland and Scotland in the seventeenth century. In small villages and rural areas, folks dressed up in costumes and got rowdy. Why? Well, since the first few centuries of the Christian era, Halloween in those Celtic lands had a reputation of being the night when ghosts, witches, demons, and faeries were free to wander. That made it the perfect time to get away with a bit of mischief-making. People also wore masks to avoid being recognized by the wandering ghosts. Men and boys hid behind masks or rubbed charcoal all over their faces, then ran around making noise, throwing trash, and harassing their neighbors (playing tricks, in other words). Sometimes they chased pretty girls or went begging for gifts (the treats). Girls joined in the fun on occasion, always in disguise. But mostly it was a night of male bonding, showing off, and trying to outdo each other.

By the end of the nineteenth century, more than two million men and women had emigrated from Ireland to live in North American cities. Quite naturally, they tended to live near other Irish families in the same neighborhoods, and they celebrated the holidays the way they had in the Old Country. On Halloween, that meant dressing up in disguises and running around, dumping trash in the streets or begging for gifts. Among more genteel families, it meant costume parties—a practice that quickly became popular with all city folks.

In the United States, it didn't take long for storekeepers to realize they could make a profit off this curious custom. By the late eighteen hundreds, shops were selling masks throughout October for children and adults. By the twentieth century, Halloween was celebrated coast to coast, and families, schools, and churches all hosted costume parties. The first citywide Halloween celebration happened in Anoka, Minnesota, in 1921.

The long-term result? Halloween is big business. About 60 percent of all Americans celebrate Halloween, and one-third of them bought costumes in 2007. Those people each spent an average of about thirty-eight dollars on their fancy frocks—for a total of $1.82 billion.

Q Why do Western languages read left to right and Eastern languages right to left?

A Go ahead—ask any lefthander why we in the West read and write from left to right. We're betting that the answer will be that it's because we live in a world that's designed for the right-handed majority.

Maybe there's some truth to that. Remember how the lefty kids in your class in grade school did that awkward-looking twisty thing with their left hands while they wrote? And watch lefthanders try to write on a dry-erase board—if they aren't careful, their writing hand smudges what they've just written. There's just one fly in the ointment with that theory: Hebrew and Arabic languages, which also are written and read horizontally, go right to left. And the people who speak those languages aren't any less likely to be right-handed.

The fact is, writing systems are so old and so varied that no one can say with any certainty how they ended up the way they are. In Egyptian hieroglyphs, the direction of a line is determined by the direction the characters are facing. If the characters face left, the line is read from right to left, and vice versa.

And sometimes ancient languages were written *boustrophedon* style, meaning that the lines alternated; one line would go from right to left and then the next would go from left to right. (*Boustrophedon* is a word with Greek origins that means "to turn like oxen," as in plowing. You plow one row in one direction, and then you turn around and plow the next row in the opposite direction.) The early Greek alphabet (a direct ancestor of Western alphabets that are used today) was originally written from right to left, then *boustrophedon* style, and then eventually left to right.

Most of the major Eastern languages were influenced by Chinese. Traditional Chinese writing goes from top to bottom, with the columns progressing from right to left. Why the writing goes from top to bottom is not known, but right-handedness may have had an influence on the right-to-left progression. Early Chinese calligraphers wrote on scrolls; a right-handed calligrapher would hold a brush in the right hand while writing and use the left hand to hold and roll open the scroll. A wise left-handed calligrapher probably found another line of work.

Horizontal text has become more common in the East, particularly in China in recent years. Computer technology has contributed to this change. Ever try to write vertically with your word-processing software? You'd need the patience of a left-handed Chinese calligrapher.

Q Why is Christmas on December 25?

A Is December 25 the day Jesus was born? Not likely. The Bible makes no mention of the birthdate of Jesus. And for the first two centuries of Christianity, observing the birthdays of martyrs was strongly discouraged—in part because celebrating birthdays was a pagan custom.

In its early years, the Roman Catholic Church gave little consideration to the precise day on which Jesus was born. Early in the fourth century, however, it apparently discovered a motivation to fix the date. According to the most popular and plausible explanation, the Roman Catholic Church chose December 25 in order to trump competing traditions.

Many dates for the birth had been proposed over the years. In AD 221, historian Sextus Julius Africanus wrote a lengthy world history that included Christianity and calculated December 25 as the day Jesus was born. The Roman Catholic Church found that this date suited its purposes, since December 25 was already set aside for pagan festivals that were popular among Romans. Among these were *natalis solis invicti* ("day of the birth of the unconquered sun") and the birthday of Mithra, or Mithras, a solar god also known as the Iranian god of light, who was worshipped by many Roman soldiers.

Generally, it's acknowledged that AD 336 was the year that the Roman Catholic Church established December 25 as the date of

Jesus's birth. If the goal was to supplant pagan holidays with a Christian one, the decision clearly was a smashing success. As any Yule-season shopper can attest, it's really hard to find a "Merry Mithras" card these days.

Q Why is Friday the thirteenth unlucky?

A It's perhaps the most pervasive superstition in North America, Western Europe, and Australia. In fact, if you're like lots of other fearful folks, you won't take a flight, get married, sign a contract, or even leave your house on this most doomed of days.

What exactly makes Friday the thirteenth more luckless than, say, Tuesday the fifth? The answer is deeply rooted in biblical, mythological, and historical events.

Friday and the number thirteen have been independently sinister since ancient times—maybe since the dawn of humans. Many biblical scholars say that Eve tempted Adam with the forbidden apple on a Friday. Traditional teachings also tell us that the Great Flood began on a Friday, the Temple of Solomon was destroyed on a Friday, and Abel was slain by Cain on a Friday.

For Christians, Friday and the number thirteen are of the utmost significance. Christ was crucified on Friday, and thirteen is the number of people who were present at the Last Supper. Judas, the disciple who betrayed Jesus, was the thirteenth member of the party to arrive.

Groups of thirteen may be one of the earliest and most concrete taboos associated with the number. It's believed that both the ancient Vikings and Hindus thought it unpropitious to have thirteen people gather together in one place. Up until recently, French socialites known as *quatorziens* (fourteeners) made themselves available as fourteenth guests to spare dinner parties from ominous ends.

Some trace the infamy of the number thirteen back to ancient Norse culture. According to mythology, twelve gods were invited to a banquet, when in walked an uninvited thirteenth guest—Loki, the god of mischief. Loki tricked the blind god Hod into throwing a spear of mistletoe at Balder, the beloved god of light. Balder fell dead, and the whole Earth turned dark.

In modern times, thirteen continues to be a number to avoid. About 80 percent of high-rise buildings don't have a thirteenth floor, many airports skip gate number thirteen, and you won't find a room thirteen in some hospitals and hotels.

How did Friday and thirteen become forever linked as the most disquieting day on the calendar? It just may be that Friday was unlucky and thirteen was unlucky, so a combination of the two was simply a double jinx. However, one theory holds that all this superstition came not as a result of convergent taboos, but of a single historical event.

On Friday, October 13, 1307, King Philip IV of France ordered the arrest of the revered Knights Templars. Tortured and forced to confess to false charges of heresy, blasphemy, and wrongdoing, hundreds of knights were burned at the stake. It's said that sympathizers of the Templars then condemned Friday the thirteenth as the most evil of days.

No one has been able to document if this eerie tale is indeed the origin of the Friday the thirteenth superstition. And really, some scholars are convinced that it's nothing more than a phenomenon created by twentieth-century media. So sufferers of paraskevidekatriaphobia (a pathological fear of Friday the thirteenth), take some comfort—or at least throw some salt over your shoulder.

Q Why are broomsticks associated with witches?

A Brooms and witches go together like—well, let's just call it a "special relationship."

Wicca, a type of witchcraft or a "nature religion," is still very much alive today. Its practitioners are known as Wiccans. Your average twenty-first-century Wiccan—when not surfing the Web, listening to Stevie Nicks on the iPhone, or chauffeuring the kids off to soccer practice in the Navigator—still uses a broom from time to time when performing the rituals of witchcraft. In addition to its handy dust-busting qualities, the broom is a tool that sweeps negativity and impurities out of areas where Wiccan rituals take place.

For hundreds of years, the broom has played this role in the practice of witchcraft. But there are some researchers who believe that the broom's original connection with witches was a little more, shall we say, personal. It's important to remember whom we're talking about here: They were witches, not Girl Scouts.

Some evidence suggests that women of yore who were accused of being witches were actually under the influence of hallucinogens. Those poor souls in Salem, Massachusetts, who were hanged in 1692 for being witches may have been reacting to a poisonous fungus called ergot that made its way into their bread. Ergot grows on rye in cool, damp weather, and when ingested, it has effects similar to those of LSD. According to this theory, the victims' ergot-inspired fits and convulsions, along with the visions they reported, were enough to freak out their neighbors and inspire accusations of witchery.

But accidental poisoning was not the only cause of hallucinations among supposed witches. Some appear to have been quite proactive in the whole affair, purposefully embarking on mind-expanding trips by consuming certain substances or by applying certain ointments. Of course, for the psychoactive ingredients in a hallucinogenic ointment to work, they have to enter the blood stream, which can only happen via the body's mucous membranes. In other words, if you don't want to eat it, you've got to put it . . . *down there.*

In his 1973 book *Hallucinogens and Shamanism*, Michael J. Harner documents a fourteenth-century example of this less-than-hygienic practice. It seems that a woman accused of witchcraft was known to have "greased a staffe" with ointment and administered said "staffe" to a certain lady-specific part of her body, with rousing results. According to this line of thinking, a witch's broomstick may have originally served the same purpose as the "staffe"—a handy applicator for hallucinogenic drugs. And what better way to escape the drudgery of housework?

Next Halloween, take a gander at those creepy green-skinned

witches riding on their broomsticks, and you'll notice that they all seem to be sporting that same lascivious-looking grin...

Q How did the days of the week get their names?

A Just like our language itself, the English words for the days of the week embody a hodgepodge of influences. Some of our names came from the ancient Babylonians and were retained by the Romans. The rest were coined by the Anglo-Saxons, and you have our permission to blame these Germanic settlers of fifth-century Britain for all of the times that you misspelled "Wednesday" when you were a kid.

When the Babylonians established the seven-day week, they named the first day after the sun and the second after the moon. The next five days were named for the five planets of which they were aware.

They had looked to their gods when labeling the planets, and so they named the third day of the week for Mars, the god of war; the fourth for Mercury, god of merchants and messenger of the gods; the fifth for Jupiter, god of the sky, who brought rain and lightning; the sixth for Venus, goddess of love; and the last day of the week for Saturn, god of seed. The Romans admired the Babylonians' style. They retained the custom of days named for heavenly bodies and their representative deities, and took along their calendar on a four-hundred-year visit to England. When finally the Romans skedaddled back to Italy, in barged the Anglo-Saxons.

The Anglo-Saxons were so occupied with pillaging that they found time to rename only four of the seven days—they retained the sun, moon, and Saturn monikers. For the rest, the Anglo-Saxons, like those before them, turned to their gods. Interestingly, they endeavored to identify each of their gods with its Roman predecessor.

So for the third day of the week, the Anglo-Saxons turned to *Tiw*, their god of war. For the fourth day, they chose *Woden*, the supreme deity. The fifth day went to *Thor*, god of thunder. And the sixth was named for their god of love, *Frigg*. (Yes, Frigg.)

Variant spellings exist, but, basically, what the Anglo-Saxons called *sunnan daeg* is now Sunday. *Monan daeg* is now Monday. *Tiwes daeg* evolved into Tuesday. *Wodnes daeg* (which didn't evolve enough) became Wednesday. *Thorsdagr* is Thursday. *Frigedaeg* is Friday. And *Saeterdag* is Saturday. And you now also have our permission to declare, "Thank Frigg it's Friday!"

Q Who read the first riot act?

A These days, you can "read the riot act" to someone using whatever types of profanity and scolding you like—there's no wrong way to do it. Originally, however, a person was required to say something very specific.

In 1714, the British government passed the Riot Act, empowering authorities to legally subdue unruly crowds. Then, as today, distinguishing a gang of rioters from a simple group of angry people was often subjective. The central idea of the Riot Act was to erase any confusion by effectively absolving soldiers and policemen of blame if they resorted to violence.

As soon as a magistrate finished reading the precise wording of a proclamation that referenced the Riot Act to a crowd of twelve or more people, the group was required to disperse or face the consequences. Regardless of whether the assemblage was doing anything illegal, failure to disperse within an hour was punishable by death. On the upside, however, rioters had a shot at getting off scot-free if the magistrate didn't read the passage exactly right. The ordinance remained on the books until 1973, though by that time it had not been enacted for decades.

If you want to authentically chew out some rabble rousers at your fraternity house, your daughter's soccer game, your office Christmas party, or anywhere else, we suggest that you read them the original Riot Act proclamation: "Our sovereign Lord of the King chargeth and commandeth all persons, being assembled, immediately to disperse themselves, and peaceably to depart to their habitations, or to their lawful business, upon pains contained in the act made in the first year of King George, for preventing tumults and riotous assemblies. God save the King." Season with profanity to taste.

Q Why does the U.S. president pardon a turkey each Thanksgiving?

A George H. W. Bush knows the answer, because he started the tradition. In 1989, he granted a presidential pardon to a turkey. Perhaps he was feeling benevolent, or maybe he wished to make the two hundredth presidential Thanksgiving proclamation memorable. Maybe Bush just liked the bird...or disliked roast turkey. It might have been to please the many children who had come to watch the National Turkey Federation deliver the bird to the White House. Whatever the reason, every president since has pardoned a turkey before Thanksgiving Day.

Many turkey observers claim that the tradition began earlier. In 1963, John F. Kennedy announced that he would not eat the turkey he received. "We'll just let this one grow," he lightheartedly told reporters before returning the fifty-five-pound bird to the farm. Newspapers reported it as a "pardon," but subsequent presidents didn't follow Kennedy's lead.

Some sources, including the White House Web site, credit Harry Truman with starting the pardon tradition in 1947. But the Truman Library disagrees, saying that 1947 was merely the first year that the National Turkey Federation began to provide birds to the White House. The buck may have stopped at Truman's desk, but not the axe.

Abraham Lincoln might have been the first president to pardon a turkey, but it didn't trigger a tradition. In the middle of the Civil War, Lincoln proclaimed the first official Thanksgiving holiday. Thanksgiving had been observed since the days of the Pilgrims, but different parts of the country celebrated it on different days. Lincoln took advice from Sarah Josepha Hale, editor of a popular magazine, *Godey's Lady's Book*: She had urged him to select a specific day for the holiday. In October 1863, Lincoln signed a proclamation that designated the last Thursday in November as a national day of thanksgiving and praise.

Lincoln's proclamation is a fact, but there's more to the turkey part of the story. It seems Lincoln's youngest son, Tad, adopted a turkey named Jack (Tom, in some tellings) and trained the bird to eat from his hand and follow him around. When the holiday approached and Tad learned that the turkey was fated to a dinner platter, he panicked. The boy burst into a cabinet meeting to plead for Jack's life. Lincoln responded with a reprieve.

In any event, turkeydom had to wait 126 years for another Republican, George Herbert Walker Bush, to free a gobbling White House guest from the axe and begin a tradition that's stuck. We are a sentimental bunch—we like to think that he did it for the kiddies.

Q Why is 666 the sign of the devil?

A No, this question wasn't lifted from an Iron Maiden song. Like most reliable information on the subject, the connection between the devil and the number 666 comes from the Bible. And if you were a regular at Sunday school, you might rightfully suspect that the explanation originates from the zaniest book of the Bible, the Book of Revelation.

The New Testament saved most of its craziness for its final act, in which we see Satan rise to power and destroy the world, only to have Christ come back and pulverize him at the last second. In chapter thirteen (how's that for spooky?) of the book, we learn that an integral part of Satan's power-grab is sending an emissary to Earth who will force its inhabitants to worship the devil. The chapter goes on to say that all who pledge allegiance to this emissary must wear his mark on their hands or foreheads or else risk getting shut out of the new evil-topia.

Finally, at verse eighteen, we get this tidbit (depending on your translation): "Wisdom is needed here; one who understands can calculate the number of the beast, for it is a number that stands for a person. His number is six hundred and sixty-six." Thus, the number of both the devil and the Antichrist is revealed to be 666.

Many people have noted that this fact is unusually specific for a book that otherwise deals with what are presumably symbols, such as dragons coming out of the earth and fire shooting from the sky. As with the interpretation of the Book of Revelation in general, there has been a lot of debate about the precise meaning of this number.

On one side, there is the lunatic fringe, which ascribes the sign of the beast to whichever public figure has raised its ire. In the 1980s, for example, some malcontents pointed out that President Reagan's full name—Ronald Wilson Reagan—is composed of three six-letter groupings.

A more sane theory attributes the number 666 to the Roman emperor Nero. Nero blamed the Christians for the infamous burning of Rome in the first century AD, and consequently started a brutal campaign of persecution against the fledgling religion. It is believed that the author of the Book of Revelation, John the Apostle, was attempting to send a coded message to his fellow Christians to give them hope that Nero's tyranny would soon come to an end.

To ensure that only other Christians would understand his message, John used Hebrew numerology. John chose Hebrew because it is the language of Judaism, the religion that Christianity grew out of after the arrival of Christ. In Hebrew, each letter corresponds with a number. The letters/numbers from Nero's full name in Hebrew, Neron Qeisar, add up to—you guessed it—666.

Essentially, John was telling his readers that Nero would be deposed, the persecution of the Christians would end, and that

Christ would return to start the Rapture. We're still waiting on John's third prediction to come true, but as a lesser light, Meatloaf, once said, "Two out of three ain't bad."

Q How did Murphy get his own law?

A Murphy's Law holds that if anything can go wrong, it will. Not surprisingly, the most widely circulated story about the origin of Murphy's Law involves a guy named Murphy.

In 1949, Captain Edward A. Murphy, an engineer at Edwards Air Force Base in California, was working on Project M3981. The objective was to determine the level of sudden deceleration a pilot could withstand in the event of a crash. It involved sending a dummy or a human subject (possibly also a dummy) on a high-speed sled ride that came to a sudden stop and measuring the effects.

George E. Nichols, a civilian engineer with Northrop Aircraft, was the manager of the project. Nichols compiled a list of "laws" that presented themselves during the course of the team's work. For example, Nichols's Fourth Law is, "Avoid any action with an unacceptable outcome."

These sled runs were repeated at ever-increasing speeds, often with Dr. John Paul Stapp, an Air Force officer, in the passenger seat. After one otherwise-flawless run, Murphy discovered that one of his technicians had miswired the sled's transducer, so no data had been recorded. Cursing his subordinate, Murphy remarked, "If there is any way to do it wrong, he'll find it." Nichols added this little gem to his list, dubbing it Murphy's Law.

Not long after, Stapp endured a run that subjected him to forty Gs of force during deceleration without substantive injury. Prior to Project M3981, the established acceptable standard had been eighteen Gs, so the achievement merited a news conference. Asked how the project had maintained such an impeccable safety record, Stapp cited the team's belief in Murphy's Law and its efforts to circumvent it. The law, which had been revised to its current language before the news conference, was quoted in a variety of aerospace articles and advertisements, and gradually found its way into the lexicon of the military and of pop culture.

It's important to note that "laws" that are remarkably similar to Murphy's—buttered bread always lands face down; anything that can go wrong at sea will go wrong, sooner or later—had been in circulation for at least a hundred years prior to Project M3981. But even if Edward Murphy didn't break new ground when he cursed a technician in 1949, it's his "law" we quote when things go wrong, and that's all right.

Q Why would anyone want to be a devil's advocate?

A Any plan that can't survive scrutiny deserves to fail, and it's the role of the devil's advocate to ferret out the flaws and shine a light on them. This isn't being needlessly argumentative. It's a hallowed responsibility—some might say a sacred one.

Nonetheless, it can be a thankless job. When it comes to exposing foibles, there's a fine line between an honorable adversary and a horse's ass. But what's the devil got to do with it?

During the Renaissance, the Catholic Church needed a few good skeptics. In 1587, Pope Sixtus V created a judicial procedure for canonizing saints. Canonization required proof that the nominee had performed at least two miracles. One priest was chosen to present arguments against conferring sainthood—his task was to examine evidence thoroughly and note any sign that the miracles in question were not of a divine nature and could be explained by natural causes. To many Catholics, this was like taking Satan's side against faith and religious belief—it was like being the devil's advocate.

To its credit, the Vatican considered the role to be one of distinction and honor. The official title of the "devil's advocate" was *Promoter Fidei* ("Promoter of the Faith"). By challenging the faith, the advocate was actually strengthening it and, in the process, weeding out the less than saintly. One priest, Prospero Lambertini, worked as *Promoter Fidei* for twenty years; he then won a big promotion and ruled as Pope Benedict XIV from 1740 to 1758. Pope John Paul II eliminated the role of the devil's advocate in 1983. It was a controversial decision that left many Catholics wondering if the church had lowered the bar for sainthood.

The merits of a devil's advocate extend beyond religious matters, of course. Brazilian business consultant and mathematician Marcial Losada studies how groups make decisions, and he values the role of the devil's advocate. Losada notes, for example, that if no one at a marketing meeting likes a new product, but everyone goes along with it anyway in order to please the boss, the product is likely doomed. A new gizmo that is unanimously beloved is just as likely to fail, he says, if no one in the group steps up to scrutinize it for flaws before it goes to market.

Being a mathematician, Losada has reduced the dilemma to a

formula called the "Losada Line." Basically, according to Losada's theory, every decision-making group needs a positive-to-negative ratio of almost three-to-one to succeed. In other words, for roughly every three yea-sayers, a business needs one naysayer as a reality check. So if you're a devil's advocate, stand up and be counted. Consider it your sacred duty.

Chapter 11
WHO DUN IT?

Q Who wrote the first autobiography?

A Saint Augustine of Hippo, back in the fourth century AD. And just what was it that made Augustine's story so memorable that he wanted to share it with the world? We'll tell you.

Augustine was born in present-day Algeria, in Africa. As a young man, he joined the Manichean religion, which was a spiritual movement from the Middle East that blended elements of Christianity with Buddhism and other ancient religions of the East. In his late twenties, Augustine became disillusioned with the Manichean philosophy, and he was baptized into the Christian church at age thirty-three. This was a great relief to his mother Monica, who had tried to raise him as a Christian and had long pleaded with him to convert. She later joined him in the Catholic sainthood.

About ten years after Augustine's conversion, he wrote his autobiography as a series of thirteen books, collectively called the *Confessions*. While his greatest achievements were still ahead of him, the *Confessions* detail Augustine's childhood and wayward youth, and then address his conversion to the Christian path.

As he grew older, Augustine was not noted for his tolerance—he mercilessly sought to stamp out competing Christian sects, for example—but he was quite the bon vivant in his youth. He enjoyed plays and other entertainment, fine living, and the fairer sex. He fathered a child by his live-in girlfriend, a concubine who was sent off to a monastery shortly before Augustine became a Christian. Augustine never told his readers her name, but he treasured their son, Adeodatus, until the boy's untimely death at age sixteen.

Augustine's own personality came through clearly in his writings. He worried about everything, found fault with himself even after he converted to Christianity, and constantly dissected his motives and beliefs. After finishing his autobiography, Augustine became a bishop and wrote *The City of God*, a classic work of Catholic philosophy. He died at age seventy-six, and thanks to his autobiographical works, we know all about the life he lived.

Q Who invented the car?

A The car as we know it today was invented by Karl Benz, who distilled centuries of accumulated wisdom, added a dose of original thinking, and unleashed upon the world the 1886 Benz Patent Motorwagen.

"Unleashed" is a strong word to describe the debut of a three-

wheel contraption with nine-tenths of a horsepower and a top
speed of 9.3 miles per hour. But the machine that trundled over the
cobblestones of Mannheim, Germany, on
July 3, 1886, was the first self-propelled
vehicle to employ a gasoline-powered
internal combustion engine as part of a
purpose-built chassis—the basic definition
of the modern automobile.

Something so momentous seldom occurs without a qualifier,
however—and so it is with the Benz Patent Motorwagen.

For Karl Benz, the qualifier was another vehicle that first ran under
its own power in 1886, just sixty miles away in Cannstatt, Germany.
It was the inventive handiwork of partners Gottlieb Daimler and
Wilhelm Maybach. Their machine also used a gas-burning single-
cylinder engine, but it was mounted on a horse-type carriage.
Daimler's carriage was specially constructed by a Stuttgart
coachbuilder for this purpose, and had the four-wheel layout that
eventually became standard practice.

But when forced to decide, historians give the edge to Benz as the
"inventor" of the automobile. His patent was issued first (in January
1886); his Motorwagen was in operation at least a month before
Daimler and Maybach's; and vitally, Benz's three-wheeler was not
a horseless carriage but an entirely new type of vehicle, the marker
for a new age of mobility.

Others quickly followed. The Duryea brothers, Charles and Frank,
of Springfield, Massachusetts, put America on gas-powered wheels
with their motorized carriage in September 1893. Henry Ford's first

car, the experimental Quadracycle, sputtered to life in Detroit in June 1896.

By 1901, enough tinkerers had walked in the footsteps of Benz and Daimler that car building was a full-fledged industry. As for those two German pioneers, they never met face to face, but the rival companies they formed became tightly laced. Daimler proved to be the more successful carmaker. He was quicker to develop his machines, and they entranced a wealthy and colorful Austrian named Emil Jellinek. Jellinek placed large orders for Daimler automobiles, became a member of the company's board, and wielded enough influence to insist that its cars be named for his ten-year-old daughter, Mercedes.

Weathering tough times after World War I, the Daimler and Benz companies formed a syndicate to market their products, and when they merged in 1926, they created a company that combined the names of their autos, which honored the inventor of the car, along with the daughter of Emil Jellinek: Mercedes-Benz.

Q Who made Greenwich, England, the world's official timekeeper?

A Cosmopolitan globetrotters like us are always complaining that they never know the time in whatever city they've jetted to for lunch that day. It's understandable: Time zones *are* a little bewildering. But it could be worse—and before 1884, it was. That's the year an international committee established the world's modern time zones. For some reason, though, it opted to make Greenwich, England, the system's starting point.

Timekeeping hasn't always been as precise as it is today. For much of human history, time was largely a matter of estimation based on the position of the sun. But over the centuries, more accurate timepieces were developed; by the nineteenth century, clocks were keeping accurate time to within a fraction of a second. This was great, except that nobody could agree on what time to set the clocks to. Time was local-centric rather than universal—folks set their clocks based on the position of the sun over their particular locales, leading to slightly different times in different parts of the country. Travelers, then, had to adjust their timepieces whenever they reached a new destination.

The rise of the railway system in the nineteenth century increasingly exposed this problem. With every city keeping its own time, railroad companies were incapable of maintaining any semblance of a schedule, leading to utter havoc in rail travel: Passengers missed trains or connections because their watches were set to different times than those of the railways. Nineteenth- century train stations were confused messes that resembled O'Hare International Airport.

It became clear that something needed to be done. By the 1850s England's railways had standardized their times to London time, while France had standardized theirs to Rouen time. It was slightly more complicated in the United States, due to the nation's enormous size. But on November 18, 1883, the four time zones we Americans know and love went into effect, having been established earlier in the year by an association of railway operators that was called the General Time Convention.

This, however, didn't solve the problem of synchronizing global time. Consequently, the United States organized the International Meridian Conference in 1884, with the stated goal of selecting a global prime meridian and developing a standard "universal day." Delegates from more than two dozen countries attended the conference in Washington, D.C., and agreed that the line of longitude would pass through Greenwich, England, as the prime meridian (longitude of zero degrees) and, thus, the starting point for world time.

Why Greenwich? For hundreds of years, Greenwich had been home to the Royal Observatory; its clock was the one London used to officially set its time. By the mid-eighteen hundreds, all of the railways in England had set their timetables by Greenwich Mean Time; even before the aforementioned conference, time in England essentially had been standardized. After all, the sun had not yet set on the British Empire, and its enormous amount of international shipping was based on British-designed sea charts and schedules— charts that used Greenwich Mean Time as their foundation. For the rest of the world, it made sense to use a system that was already largely in place.

Now that we've cleared up the time zones, we've got another question: Who do we blame for Daylight Saving Time?

Q Who invented the smiley face?

A In 1963, an insurance company in Worcester, Massachusetts, merged with State Mutual Life Assurance. The employees were not happy. In the interest of soothing hurt feelings and helping the merger succeed, State Mutual embarked on a "friendship campaign."

An adman named Harvey Ball was hired to create a graphic for the campaign's button that would symbolize the spirit of optimism that management wanted to cultivate. Ball, who later admitted that he spent about ten minutes on the design, drew a circle with a smiling mouth on yellow paper. He thought he was finished but then realized that the design was ambiguous—turning it upside down made the smile a frown, which wasn't the desired message. So Ball added two dots for eyes to ensure that the button would be smile-only, submitted his creation, and was compensated for it—to the tune of forty-five dollars.

The first order was for a hundred buttons. They proved to be quite popular with the company's employees and customers; soon, they were selling in lots of ten thousand. Ball didn't trademark his design, so he didn't profit—beyond that first payday—on an idea that became a worldwide icon. But there were plenty of more enterprising people who looked at the smiley face and saw dollar signs.

In 1970, Bernard and Murray Spain of Philadelphia paired the smiley face with the slogan "Have a Happy Day" and began churning out cheap crap with this message of nauseating friend-liness. They slapped it on buttons, T-shirts, bumper stickers, posters, and anything else they could think of. Since there was no trademark, other entrepreneurs soon joined the fray, and a fad was born. By 1972, approximately fifty million smiley buttons had been produced.

In 1971, at the height of the craze, French entrepreneur Franklin Loufrani claimed that he had invented the smiley face in 1968. He later admitted to a *New York Times* reporter that he was merely the first to register it. He trademarked the image in eighty countries (not including the United States) and created the Smiley Licensing

Corporation, which has been a profitable enterprise.

Another would-be smiley tycoon was David Stern, a Seattle adman who claimed to have created the smiley face in 1967 after being inspired by the musical *Bye Bye Birdie*. Stern neglected to trademark the image, and his run for mayor of Seattle in 1993 earned him enough attention that *Seattle Weekly* reporter Bruce Barcott sought to authenticate the claim. Barcott found that Stern wasn't the inventor of the smiley face, and Stern lost his bid to become mayor, though it's unclear if it was because of the smiley-face scandal.

Incidentally, the creator of the smiley face emoticon—: -)—is Carnegie Mellon University professor Scott E. Fahlman, who suggested it in 1982 as a way to indicate a joke in the early days of computer message boards. Although perhaps not as ubiquitous as Ball's yellow circle (and not yet the subject of a postage stamp, as the original smiley face was in 1999), it certainly is helpful in determining how to interpret your weird co-worker's last e-mail.

Q Who was the real John Henry?

When John Henry was a bitty baby,
Sittin' on his pappy's knee,
He picked up a hammer and a little piece of steel,
And said, "This hammer's gonna be the death of me,
Lord, Lord, this hammer's gonna be the death of me."

A Was it the death of him? Did John Henry, that steel-driving man, really win a contest with a steam drill only to die of exhaustion and a broken heart? There seem to be as many candidates for the real John Henry as there are versions of the song.

He was African American or Irish or maybe Polish. He came from West Virginia, Alabama, North Carolina, or Georgia. He was a superman. He was every man.

Contrary to what you might think, historians do not dismiss folklore as mere myth and superstition. People who can't write often pass along history in stories and song. With this in mind, John Henry has been the subject of some pretty serious historical sleuthing.

One trail led Scott Nelson, a professor at the College of William and Mary, to the records of the Virginia State Penitentiary in Richmond. There, he found in the ledger an entry for John William Henry, a young black man from Elizabeth, New Jersey, who had been arrested on charges of larceny in 1866 and sentenced to ten years in jail. At that time, convicts were employed by the thousands to build a railroad line through Virginia to the Ohio River. According to the prison record, John Henry was among them.

Tunneling through the Allegheny Mountains was dangerous—even deadly—work. And it was slow. Collis Huntington, owner of the C&O Railroad, decided to try newfangled steam drills. Much to his disappointment, they kept breaking down on the job. Before he junked them entirely, though, his engineers begged him to give the drills one last chance to prove themselves by testing them against the men who were toiling at the Lewis Tunnel, exactly where John Henry and his work gang had been assigned.

Engineering records from 1870 reveal that, just like the song says, those early drills could not outdrive a man with a hammer in his hand. But was one of those men John Henry? And was there a big showdown? That will have to be left to our imaginations.

Why does the story continue to intrigue us more than a century later? First, it is a tale of courage and sacrifice. Second, and more important, it celebrates all the ordinary men, both black and white, who built the railroads and, by extension, America itself. Some forty thousand died in the construction of the C&O Railroad alone, and many of them were buried in unmarked graves. They may not have headstones, but they do have a song. And they all have one name: John Henry.

Q Who were Celsius and Fahrenheit?

A For two men who had so much in common, Daniel Gabriel Fahrenheit and Anders Celsius have caused a lot of confusion. Both played key roles in Europe's scientific revolution in the early eighteenth century, both were fascinated by science and mathematics, and both made lasting contributions to those fields. So what's the biggest difference between them? Thirty-two degrees.

Born in Poland, Fahrenheit (1686–1736) tried to become a merchant but found that he preferred the study of chemistry. By 1717, he was living in Holland and had established a successful glassblowing shop in The Hague. He specialized in the production of barometers and thermometers, which enabled him to combine science and business. Thermometers at the time used water or alcohol; Fahrenheit decided to use mercury instead because it doesn't expand like water when frozen or evaporate like alcohol when exposed to air.

He established the measurement of zero as the point at which a solution of salt, ice, and water stabilized. He then calibrated a scale of twelve intervals, each of which he subdivided into six points, or degrees. The freezing point of plain water became thirty-two degrees, and the average temperature of the human body was established as ninety-six degrees (later recalibrated to our familiar 98.6 degrees). We express these values today as 32°F, 98.6°F, and so on.

Meanwhile, in Uppsala, Sweden, Anders Celsius (1701–1744) was studying astronomy, publishing observations on the aurora borealis, and participating in expeditions that confirmed the shape of Earth. His travels convinced him that scientists needed a single international standard for measuring temperature.

Independent of Fahrenheit, Celsius developed his own thermometer. In 1741, he established a scale that set the boiling point of water at zero degrees and the freezing point at one hundred degrees. You read that right—the original Celsius scale was "upside down." A year after Celsius's death, the scale was reversed by Swedish botanist Carl Linnaeus and became the Celsius thermometer that we have today.

Celsius degrees were also called "degrees centigrade" because they were measured in increments from zero to one hundred. This fit with the metric system adopted by France in 1791. On May 20, 1875, seventeen European states signed the *Convention du Mètre*, an agreement that made the metric system—and the Celsius scale along with it—the official measurement standard of Europe.

The United States remains the last major nation to rely on the Fahrenheit scale, and that probably won't change anytime soon. So if your French friends say that it's in the low thirties on the Left Bank, don't pack your down jacket for April in Paris. Indeed, most of the world considers thirty-two degrees perfectly pleasant shirtsleeve weather—thirty-two degrees Celsius, that is.

The formula for conversion from Celsius to Fahrenheit is a bit tricky. One degree Celsius equals 1.8 degrees Fahrenheit. So if it's thirty degrees Celsius in Paris, multiply by 1.8, and add thirty-two to determine that it's a balmy eighty-six degrees Fahrenheit. *Bon voyage*, and leave the mittens—and Mr. Fahrenheit's thermometer—behind.

Q Who were the Goths?

A We don't mean today's multi-pierced, darkly clothed wannabe vampires or the nineteenth-century purveyors of ghost stories and mysteries. No, the original Goths lived in the days of the Roman Empire.

Roman historians claimed that the Goths emerged from Scandinavia, but the earliest archaeological evidence of their existence was discovered in Poland,and dates back to the first century AD—when the Roman Empire was on the rise. Over time, the Goths, a Germanic tribe, moved south; the Roman Empire, meanwhile, pushed north. The two groups met somewhere in between and fought. The Goths sacked Roman frontier cities and annihilated a Roman army, killing Emperor Decius and his son. The Romans eventually drove the Goths back, but the Goths gained a frightening reputation as barbarian bogeymen.

By the fourth century, the Goths had increased their power and had divided into several kingdoms north of the Roman Empire. The Romans saw them as Visigoths (western Goths) and Ostrogoths (eastern Goths), but there may have been more groups that were known by different names.

During the 370s, the Huns—you've heard of Attila? Yup, same guys—attacked the Goths from the east, forcing the Goths to push into the Roman Empire again. This time, having become a bit more civilized, the Goths asked permission of the Romans before crossing the Danube. Predictably, however, things turned ugly. The Romans and the Goths went to war, and another Roman Emperor—Valens— bit the dust at the Battle of Adrianople.

That Gothic War lasted six years and marked the twilight of the Roman Empire. When Rome was forced to negotiate a settlement, surrounding tribes saw that the Empire was weak. Fewer than twenty years later, the Visigoths sacked the city of Rome. They then moved west to establish a kingdom in what today is southern France and Spain; this kingdom lasted for almost three centuries.

The Ostrogoths, after years of fighting the Huns in the Balkans, more or less took over the Roman Empire after it fell. Here's how it happened: In AD 476, a barbarian named Odoacer deposed the last Roman Emperor in the west. Gothic King Theodoric the Great fought Odoacer several times and laid siege to the city of Ravenna for three years until Odoacer surrendered. At a banquet celebrating the end of the siege, Theodoric raised a toast—then killed Odoacer with his own hands and took over the Italian peninsula.

Theodoric's empire extended from Spain to the Balkans, but after his death, it fell apart. The Eastern Roman Empire attacked, and the Ostrogoths pretty much disappeared. Their former lands were conquered by other rulers.

Think about all of this the next time you're walking down the street and you pass a pale, sullen-looking person who's dressed entirely in black and has piercings galore.

Q Who were the most famous female pirates?

A "Lady pirate" may not sound like a job description our great-great-grandmothers would have gone for, but according to historians, many women did indeed pursue lives of plunder on the high seas.

One of the earliest female pirates was Artemesia of Persia, whose fleet preyed upon the city-states of Greece during the fifth century BC. The Athenians put a price of ten thousand drachmas on her head, but there's no record of anyone ever collecting it.

Teuta of Illyria (circa 230 BC) was a pirate queen who led raids against Roman ships. Another notable was Alfhild (circa the ninth century AD), a Viking princess who reportedly kept a viper for a pet and whose all-female longboat crew ravaged the Scandinavian coast. Prince Alf of Denmark captured Alfhild, but her beauty so overwhelmed him that he proposed marriage instead of beheading her, and they ruled together happily ever after. At least that's one story; there's a little blarney in every pirate yarn.

Legend has it that Grania O'Malley (1530–1603), who was captain of a pirate fleet based in Ireland, gave birth to her son Toby while at sea. The next day, blunderbuss in hand, she led her men to victory over a

Turkish warship.

Madame Ching (circa 1785–1844), perhaps the most notorious of all the pirate queens, ruled her league of two thousand ships and seventy thousand men with an iron hand—anyone who was caught stealing loot for private use was executed immediately. But she was relatively kind to some of her prisoners: For example, she ordered that captive women and children not be hung by their hair over the side of the ship.

Closer to home, Anne Bonny (1698–1782) and Mary Read (circa 1690–1721) dressed as men and served aboard pirate ships that sailed the Caribbean. They met when Mary, disguised as one James Morris, joined a crew that was commanded by Anne and her husband, Calico Jack Rackham.

One night while the men were sleeping off a rum binge below deck, Anne and Mary were left to face down a British man-of-war alone. Despite their bravery, their ship was quickly captured and the pirates were hauled off to prison. After learning that Calico Jack had received a death sentence, Anne's last words to him were: "I am sorry…but had you had fought like a man, you need not have been hanged like a dog."

Anne and Mary escaped death by "pleading their bellies," meaning they both were conveniently pregnant. Mary died in childbirth a few months later; Anne dropped from historical view. Anne is said to have married again and become a respectable matron in the city of Charleston, South Carolina. But one rumor suggests that Mary only pretended to die, and that she and Anne escaped to New Orleans, where they raised their kids and occasionally plied their former trade—fast friends and pirates of the Caribbean to the very end.

Q Did Betsy Ross really make the first American Flag?

A American history is big business. Each year tourists flock to historical sites, where they spend millions of dollars on replicas of the Declaration of Independence, ceramic busts of George Washington, lunches at fake colonial taverns, and Liberty Bell snow globes. Not that we're complaining—we love historical snow globes as much as the next patriot. But this massive tourist economy depends less on actual history and more on good stories (or myths, as some sticklers might call them).

Some of these stories are widely recognized as myths: George Washington chopping down the cherry tree, for example. But the origins of others are murkier. For example: Did Betsy Ross sew the first American flag?

For those of you who have forgotten your grade-school pageants, the Betsy Ross tale goes something like this: In May 1776, three members of the Continental Congress, including Washington himself, visited humble seamstress Betsy Ross with a secret request: They needed a flag for the soon-to-be United States of America. Betsy, who was an expert seamstress as well as a remarkable woman (she lost two husbands to the Revolution), immediately set to work creating the enduring symbol of freedom and glory. It's a great story, told and re-told in history pageants from sea to shining sea. The only problem is, it's probably not true.

Considering how thoroughly much of the struggle for independence is documented, there is surprisingly little in the historical record about the origin of the Stars and Stripes, possibly because contemporary chroniclers were more concerned with a little thing called the Revolution. In fact, nobody cared much about who sewed the first American flag until March 1870, when historian William Canby presented a paper to the Philadelphia Historical Society that proclaimed Betsy Ross as the mother of the American flag. Betsy Ross was Canby's grandmother, and his historical evidence was primarily the affidavits of his relatives and the memories of a few ancient people who were nearing senility. In absence of other definitive evidence, the public quickly latched onto Canby's claim and elevated Betsy Ross from simple seamstress to Mother of Freedom.

Nowadays, few legitimate historians support the tale, pointing out, among other things, that George Washington was probably more concerned with patching together his army than with visiting humble seamstresses to talk flag design. Historians also point out that Francis Hopkinson, a signer of the Declaration of Independence, submitted a bill to Congress requesting compensation for his design of the American flag; this is the only documented evidence of anyone claiming responsibility. Indeed, most historians—and the United States government—recognize Hopkinson as the original designer.

Still, Betsy's legend is powerful. Perhaps it's no surprise that in surveys polling American students, Betsy Ross is among the most famous non-presidential Americans in history.

Q Was there really a guy named Johnny Appleseed?

A Someone named Johnny Appleseed traipsing around in bare feet, with a tin kettle on his head. No, we're not describing the latest nut-job on a reality series. Believe it or not, there really was a man who went by the moniker Johnny Appleseed. While some of the stories about him are suspect—especially the bit about the tin kettle on his head—he is an important part of the history of the United States.

He was born John Chapman in 1774 in Leominster, Massachusetts; his father was a Minuteman who fought for the Continental Army during the Revolutionary War. Little is known about Johnny's daily life when he was growing up or when he was a young man. At about the age of twenty-six, he headed to the developing Midwest. In Pennsylvania, he picked up a load of apple seeds from cider presses and moved into what would become Ohio. There, he planted apple nurseries along streams, rivers, and creeks. Before long, his fellow pioneers started calling him Johnny Appleseed.

He was not a seed scatterer, as some people think, but rather one of the founding fathers of the nursery industry. Johnny tended to his apple nurseries and started new ones whenever he found a good spot. He didn't plant all of his seedlings for free: While he would give some away to new settlers and Native Americans, he often charged six cents for a seedling. He also accepted cornmeal or old clothes as barter if people didn't have money.

Johnny lived simply. He really did go around without shoes, slept outdoors, and most likely wore castoff clothing. But he was not poor. He donated the money he earned from his nurseries to charity or used it to further his business. Chapman spent nearly fifty years planting nursery after nursery in what is now Pennsylvania, Ohio, Indiana, Illinois, and Kentucky. Some of his trees still bear fruit.

Why apples? Johnny believed that apples would be important to the development of the Midwest, which then was mostly wilderness. Apple trees were easy to grow, and the fruit was versatile: Apples could be made into butter and cider, and could be dried and saved for use during the winter months.

Johnny's deeds made him revered along the frontier by settlers and Native Americans alike. The next time you're in a Midwest state and are about to bite into an apple, take a moment to reflect on the significance of the tasty fruit—just don't commemorate the occasion by putting a tin kettle on your head.

Q Who got the first tattoo?

A The story of the first tattoo does not involve a bachelor party. Incredible, we know.

The first tattoo was probably an accident. Not the kind of accident that leads to the name Roxie above the biceps—a real accident. Tattoos have been around for several thousand years and might have started when someone rubbed a wound with dirt, soot, or ash and noticed that the mark stayed after the injury had healed.

For the sake of giving this question a definitive answer, we turn to Iceman, who sports the oldest tats ever seen on a body. In 1991, the frozen and amazingly well-preserved remains of a Bronze Age man were found between Austria and Italy in the Tyrolean Alps. Iceman, as he was dubbed, is believed to be more than five thousand years old, and he clearly has a series of lines tattooed on his lower back, ankles, knees, and foot. It is thought that the tattoos were applied for medicinal purposes, to reduce pain.

Over time, tattoos evolved into symbols or designs that have meaning. Mummified Egyptian women dating back to 2100 BC have patterns of lines and dots on their bodies that were applied, historians believe, to enhance fertility and provide protection. All tattoos in this period were thought of as a way of connecting the body to a higher power.

When did someone finally step it up and go with something more intricate than lines and dots? That question is impossible to answer conclusively, but a Nubian mummy, circa 400 BC, has a tattoo of Bes, the Egyptian god of fertility and revelry, on her thigh. Several Egyptian paintings from this period depict dancers and musicians with Bes tattoos on their thighs.

Tattoos have gone in and out of style. In early Rome, for instance, they were decidedly out of style and were even banned among the general populace because they were thought to taint the body's purity. Back then, body ink was reserved for criminals (as a form of punishment, like a scarlet letter) and slaves (so that they could be identified if they escaped). Eventually, attitudes changed—Roman soldiers began getting tattoos after fighting a rugged army of Britons who wore their body art like badges of honor.

Today, it's hard to find a professional basketball player or a musical performer who isn't sporting ink. There are even reality shows about the studios—don't say "parlors," because it isn't cool and you'll sound like a crusty old sailor—where tattoos are applied. A Harris Interactive poll in 2008 revealed that about half of Americans between ages eighteen and twenty-nine have a tattoo. No word on how much of that ink was still fresh the morning after a bachelor—or bachelorette—party.